*"Nobody on the planet has de...
the entire history of Mötley Cr.. ...., ...ougy,
and continuously than Paul Miles. Rather than recount the story
of the most reckless musical act the world has ever seen in the
past tense, this book will guide you through every step of the way
as it all unfolded. Pulling no punches and telling no lies, Paul
Miles will reveal facts that have been covered up, forgotten, or
falsified by every previous account. Get ready to find out the real
truth behind the highest highs and lowest lows in the Crüe's
perilous kingdom of sex, drugs, and rock n' roll..."*

Steve-O, of MTV's Jackass and Wildboyz infamy

*"Chronological Crue is without a doubt the definitive Mötley
Crüe reference work. I used it extensively in writing the script of*
The Dirt *and I highly recommend it to not only fans of the band,
but anyone with an interest in the history of rock n' roll. For
contained on these sweaty pages is a treasure trove of sleazy
tidbits on not just the band but the slew of other musicians,
critics, groupies, scum sucking corporate-types, famous wives
and infamous playthings who came across their path. If Mötley
played with them, partied with them or shagged them silly, it's
here for all to see. It is a compulsive completist's dream, filled
with the sort of arcane minutia that can settle arguments, win
bets, or simply allow you to sleep after pondering for hours the
exact date of Nikki Sixx's first overdose in the back alleys of
Hammersmith. Now hurry up and buy it so Paul Miles can
finally feel as if his life has meaning."*

Rich Wilkes, screenwriter of Mötley's movie *The Dirt*

Chron· o· log· i· cal *adj.*

1. Arranged in order of time of occurrence.

Crue *n.*

2. The world's most notorious rock band - Mötley Crüe.

Collect these other Mötley Crüe books by Paul Miles:

Chronological Crue Vol. 2 - The Nineties
The complete history of Mötley Crüe in the 1990s

Chronological Crue Vol. 3 - The Naughties
The complete history of Mötley Crüe in the 2000s

Chronological Crue Vol. 4 - The Onesies
The ongoing history of Mötley Crüe in the 2010s

Mötley Crüe Down Under
On Tour with The Carnival of Sins

What Mötley Crüe Means to Me
Crüeheads Share Their Stories

Lots more in the world of Mötley Crüe at the Chronological Crue website:
   www.CrueTime.com

Chronological Crue Vol. 1 - The Eighties

THE COMPLETE HISTORY OF MÖTLEY CRÜE IN THE 1980s

Paul Miles

First edition published 2006.
This second edition, published by:

   Chronological Crue
   GPO Box 2220
   Melbourne Victoria 3001
   Australia

   Email: milestone1183@yahoo.com
   Web: www.CrueTime.com

Chronological Crue is a publishing entity of Paul Miles,
ABN 21 790 841 870

Printed with chlorine-free ink on acid-free interior paper stock, made from 30% post-consumer waste recycled material. Manufactured on-demand to reduce any excess production.

ISBN 978-1-7954-6013-2

**This book is dedicated to my loving wife and children
Sara, Louise & Benjamin**
especially for your tolerance of my Mötley Crüe fanaticism
over so many years now.

…and to the immortal Mötley Crüe
for the continuing inspiration, drama and success
that's kept me writing and sharing with fans worldwide.

Contents

FOREWORD BY

NEIL STRAUSS

I will never forget the first time I met Mötley Crüe.

It was sometime in the late '90s at an amphitheater in the American Southwest. I had been assigned to interview the band for Spin Magazine, and had flown into town that day to meet them. I arrived at the amphitheater, picked up my ticket and backstage pass, and proceeded to watch the melee on stage.

Afterward, as I walked backstage to meet the band, I heard a police officer on a radio. He was making a plan to arrest two people at the concert. Their names: Nikki Sixx and Tommy Lee. The officer was describing to his partner exactly what the pair looked like – in case they arrested the wrong members of the band. I can't remember the exact charges now except for something about kicking a security guard in the head and inciting concertgoers to bare their breasts. Or maybe they were kicking concertgoers in the head and inciting security guards to bare their breasts.

I ran backstage and saw Nikki walking out of the dressing room. I warned him that the police were about to come back and arrest them.

"You should leave now before they get here," I urged.

He laughed it off and asked if his road manager had put me up to this. Evidently, he thought it was some kind of prank.

Ten minutes later, Nikki and Tommy were in handcuffs. Tommy was wearing nothing but his tight leather stage shorts. As he was led away, a fan held up a Mötley Crüe album and asked if he would autograph it. Tommy shrugged and nodded forlornly at his handcuffs.

And that was my first encounter with Mötley Crüe: violence, nudity, betrayal, police, prison, and gallows humor. It took them all of fifteen minutes to live up to their reputation.

Likewise, I will never forget the first time I met Paul Miles.

He emailed me. Or maybe I emailed him. I can't remember which.

Sure, it's not quite as exciting as meeting Mötley Crüe. In fact, there's no comparison. But Paul has proven to be just as loyal and meaningful a friend and partner in crime.

It is people like Paul Miles who are the backbone of bands like Mötley Crüe. Because Paul, even though he wasn't at the concert described above, knows the exact date on which it took place, the city it was located in, the name of the amphitheater, and probably the attendance and ticket price. He also knows the exact charges the band was arrested on, how long they were detained, and the end result of the incident.

In short, Paul Miles knows more about Mötley Crüe than Mötley Crüe do.

He even knows the exact amount of times the word "dude" is used in *The Dirt*.

And in return, he's asked for nothing.

There are two kinds of people who surround popular bands: destructive and constructive. The former are all too numerous: they'll take a band's money, feed them drugs, turn band-mates into enemies, drive them into bankruptcy, and generally waste their time. The latter are rare. And it is in this category that Paul belongs. Given the choice, most bands would rather have a Paul Miles in their corner than a Subaru full of groupies. Because it is thanks to Paul, and these volumes here, that any order can be made out of the chaotic shit-storm that Mötley Crüe has left in its wake.

When I think of Paul, I think of a large roving eye that is constantly following the members of Mötley Crüe. Every move they make, Paul Miles knows. Every divorce they take, Paul Miles knows. Every press release they fake, Paul Miles knows. Reading these books, the entries have morphed so much since I last saw them: hundreds of newer entries have been added and older entries have been expanded and updated to create one of the most accurate, comprehensive, and engrossing chronological compendiums of any band of the era.

And Paul has done more for the band and its audience than compiling the fanthology you hold in your hands and writing liner notes to *Entertainment or Death*. For years now, Paul has been the voice representing every Mötley Crüe fan, constantly whispering in the ears of the band and its management, keeping them in touch with the needs of their audience in a world in which reality is never close at hand.

After I wrote *The Dirt* with Mötley Crüe, I did a book with Jenna Jameson, the porn star. And I searched the web everywhere for some kind of Genealogical Jenna site to help guide the process. There wasn't one. And I missed having the resource of someone like Paul Miles to correspond with and check for accuracy and integrity. So, Paul, if you ever get this Mötley Crüe thing chronologically wrapped up, I have someone new to introduce you to. She could use a fan like you. That is, as long as your wife doesn't mind.

Read more about Neil Strauss and his projects at www.neilstrauss.com

PREFACE

From the time I was born in 1969, music has always been in my life. Dad, and Mum especially, liked listening to the current popular music played on commercial radio, along with their favourite hits from the '50s and '60s. As a boy, this was the music I knew and mostly enjoyed. In 1979, I was gripped by a rock phenomenon that controlled many other kids at the time: Kiss. Their November 1980 first tour here in Australia shattered concert records and received an enormous amount of media and public attention. Although deemed too young to attend the shows, a permanent scar was left on me.

As I entered high school in the early '80s, my mates and I were still predominantly listening to chart music, with favourites including INXS, Split Enz, and Billy Joel. Seeing David Bowie live in November 1983 as my first concert gave me more of a taste and I started exploring his back catalogue. Through my early teen years I took hold of the radio dial and started listening to the stations run by Universities. This triggered my appetite for music as I was discovering alternative bands like The Cramps, Violent Femmes, The Cult, The Birthday Party, Alien Sex Fiend, and The Stooges.

Further varied listening then introduced me to all sorts of punk music and I enjoyed early English giants The Clash, The Damned, Generation X and the Sex Pistols. Whilst I loved the melodies of these bands' songs, I found myself preferring the bands with more snarl. The Dead Kennedys were one such favourite that continued to expose me to different styles. Lots of American hardcore punk bands then occupied my turntable, like Channel 3, Black Flag, Circle Jerks, and Fear. So much so that in 1986 a friend and I were spending some late nights at a University radio station, playing hardcore and other punk music over the airwaves. I left High School with my best marks in English and a fail in History!

I continued to enjoy exploring punk music listening to more English punk bands like Subhumans, The Exploited, Angelic Upstarts, The Partisans, and the Clay Records trio: English Dogs, Discharge, and G.B.H. It was these latter three I liked the most, and when I sang in my first band called Barbary Corsairs in 1987, I belted-out some versions of our favourite songs from these bands. Coupled with punked Rose Tattoo, Devo and Sixto Rodriguez covers amongst our set of originals, we found ourselves frequently opening for local act Cremator.

Cremator were the first speed metal band in hometown Perth, Australia, influenced by the likes of Slayer, Possessed, Dark Angel and Metallica. I found myself getting into this heavier music more and more. Slayer's *Reign in Blood* and Metallica's *Master of Puppets* wore thin on my turntable as well as discs from bands like Whiplash, Exodus, Anthrax, Onslaught, Death Angel and Death. I loved listening to these bands but after a while found myself preferring a slower pace with a heavier groove. Enter Black Sabbath, Saint Vitus, Trouble and some Led Zeppelin.

As 1988 came around, The Cult's *Electric* was all over the night scene and Guns N' Roses' *Appetite for Destruction* was just breaking ground in Australia. It was not only the hard rock sound that grabbed me but the image and style these bands had. My discovery of these bands and a re-discovery of Kiss had me exploring more hard rock. By the time early 1989 came around I was digging up vinyl on more of these new hard rock bands. I remember buying import records of Skid Row, Faster Pussycat, Dangerous Toys and Poison, and turning many friends on to them. I also began collecting videos and audios of my favourite bands around this time, as it was near impossible to obtain anything but standard commercial releases in Perth – the most isolated capital city in the world.

It was at this time I met my wife-to-be Sara, through a mutual friend from the punk days. We clicked instantly and it was Sara that then introduced me to Aerosmith and Mötley Crüe's *Too Fast for Love* album, which we partied to for many, many months on end. My path somehow never previously crossed with *Too Fast for Love*, nor *Shout at the Devil* and *Theatre of Pain* in their day. I recall seeing the *Girls, Girls, Girls* record in a store prior to this but never picked it up.

For my next birthday, Sara had a pair of black leather pants with a lace-up crotch made for me by the ex-wife of Sex Pistol Glen Matlock and they were just like Vince's from the *Too Fast for Love* album cover. I remember making myself a handcuff belt and screen-printing Crüe t-shirts for friends and myself.

Later in 1989, I obtained a 'hot off the press' bootleg video of the Crüe's performance at the Moscow Peace Festival. If I wasn't hooked before I certainly was now. That video was played over and over and over. When *Dr. Feelgood* was released soon after, the Crüe was building mainstream popularity in Australia. When they toured Australia in late March-early April 1990 (the one and only time until Dec 2005) they did not play on our west coast. Sara and I were unemployed at the time and preparing for our wedding in a few months, so we had to sit back and hear stories from people we knew that were able to make the 3,500km journey across the country to see them. Crüe-fever died down in Australia for many years after that tour but it had hooked lots of other Aussies.

So, fast forward through more years of listening to hard rock and metal, I then had my first exposure to the Internet in 1994 when the company I was working for at the time connected. I had an email address and a web browser, and I was away. There were only really two small Mötley Crüe sites on the 'net back then and these were among the sites I found myself visiting most often, hoping for news on what the band members were up to and other fresh content. I also enjoyed the variety of Kiss websites online back then.

After reading various online FAQ's covering all sorts of topics, I realised there was no FAQ for Mötley Crüe. This realisation coupled with the desire to actively contribute to the Internet gave me the initial concept and idea for a website. I had often considered starting a Mötley Crüe fanzine (being aware of the role of fanzines from my punk days) but I held back due to my limited funds for printing and distribution, so I saw a website as the best way for me to get involved. There was no Mötley history available online back then as well, so I decided this would be the unique focus for my website, as I found the stories of their misadventures to be intriguing and so very rock 'n' roll. I saw no point in just duplicating information or copying ideas from other Mötley sites like so many other websites were doing (and still continue to do). I wanted my website to be a timeline of the Crüe's history and in doing so it would answer the FAQ's fans have about them, their music and their lives; so I came up with the name Chronological Crue.

With no idea of how to build a website, I realised I first needed to have all my content in electronic format. So early in 1995 I began entering as much information into my word processor as possible. Mountains of magazines, books, newspaper clippings, video tapes, audio tapes, etc. were scoured for dates and facts to be entered. Rather than copying articles and information as it appeared, I stripped the editorialised information back to the bare facts and completely re-wrote the text in my own style and words. It was quite amazing just how much embellishment was written around these facts by journalists, but I understand that's their craft. The many inconsistencies I found were also eye-opening and I have always strived to present the most accurate version of events that I can.

The content is written in British English (I'm an Australian, descendent of convicts!) as a third-person narrative in the present tense chronological, so readers can ride the ups and downs as the band's amazing story unfolds.

Towards the end of 1995, or early 1996, I felt I had enough content but still didn't possess the technical skills to turn it into a website. I approached the webmaster of the official Mötley website hoping to come to an arrangement for my history to be published on that site. For one reason and another, nothing eventuated there, so I decided I'd do it all myself.

I also wanted the website to be a Mötley museum of sorts, so when reading the history, a simple click on linked information would display an image of the event as well. Many images were scanned from my personal Crüe collection of Mötley merchandise that had been steadily growing over the years. Throughout 1996, I constructed the website locally on my laptop in the format intended. I wanted to keep my site basic without so many of the whistles and bells, yet still being able to present a professional looking site. I recognised that depth of content and frequent updates would be the key to the site's success, as that was what I appreciated and looked for in websites generally.

In the latter half of 1996 with the information complete, the issue of hosting the website forced me to restructure much of the work I'd done. Due to limited server space and a lack of ongoing funds to invest in hosting, since the site provided no income for such expenses, I had to remove the linked historical images prior to uploading the site to its home at Australia's then-largest ISP, OzEmail. When it came time to choose a username for the hosting account at my ISP, 'cruekiss' seemed the obvious choice (my favourite two bands.)

So after many months of work over the last two years, the site was ready to go live in the early part of 1997. On January 16, a teaser awareness campaign began directing fans to a singular introductory page that invited them to come back for the launch on January 27, 1997 – the day Vince Neil was to re-unite with the Crüe on stage at the American Music Awards. The website became fully accessible that Monday morning so Mötley fans could spend the day reading through the band's past, then later that evening witness the beginning of a new chapter in Mötley Crüe history.

The Chronological Crue website has since gone from strength to strength, being featured in many print publications around the world and having its pages viewed many millions of times. Major US music networks MTV and VH1 have drawn upon and credited the site for production of their TV programs on Mötley Crüe. The site continued to constantly update fans on all the latest on Mötley Crüe and its band members – both past and present – for the next twenty years!

Fans from all over the globe constantly show their appreciation of my work, time invested, and experience provided for them. They are often shocked to find out that there is no team of people working on the site and it's just me, in what time 'spare time' I've been able to dedicate.

Over the years, I received many, many emails from fans around the world suggesting that Chronological Crue should be turned into a book, so they can use it as a reference source for all the times they are not online; whether it is as a handy lounge room fact source to settle a bet between mates, something to read on a flight or holiday, or simply for the enjoyment of reading a good book.

The first edition of this Chronological Crue book series was published in 2006 and was available for many years until it went out of print. It didn't take long for the emails to start arriving again, with fans (and often, their partners) asking where they could get their hands on a copy, or asking when the series would be re-published. Well, the long wait is over, as I'm now pleased and proud to make this updated second edition of the series available early in 2019.

The Chronological Crue website at CrueTime.com and this second edition series of Mötley history books are my SHOUT for all you Crüeheads worldwide. Enjoy them!

Long live Mötley Crüe… 'til death do us part.

Rock on,
Paul Miles

1950, DECEMBER 18

RANDY CASTILLO

Randolph Frank Castillo is born in Albuquerque, New Mexico, USA on this Monday. His mother Margaret is Spanish, while his father Frank was born to Mexican and Native American parents. Randy is one of five children, having four sisters, Frances, Marilyn, Phyllis and Christine, who all play music.

Childhood

His musical career begins when he plays drums in his elementary school marching band. He then plays trumpet for about four years, including performing in his father's band called Los Aguilas, which is Spanish for The Eagles. With his father on guitar, they perform Mariachi music at local weddings and parties, but he soon loses interest when he realises the kind of bands he likes don't have trumpet players. He decides he wants a drum kit instead, especially after seeing The Beatles rock on the Ed Sullivan Show in early February 1964. His father refuses to buy one for him, thinking he will also lose interest with it, as he did with the trumpet.

Teen Years

At fourteen years of age, Randy's youngest sister is born and on the same day his mother buys him his first drum set, with her last paycheck from working as a secretary for the Albuquerque Public Schools, following Randy's pleads over the last two years. The small Ludwig kit has one high hat and one symbol, and Randy plays it nonstop in their garage.

Two weeks later he is asked to join a local rhythm and blues band called The Sheltons, one of the city's most popular bands, but he is kicked out after a few months when their old drummer Toby re-joins, who had quit before they asked Randy to play for them. This devastates Randy but inspires him to take lessons at Luchetti's Music with Nick Luchetti, at the time one of the best instructors in the city, if not the state, and owner of the shop where his drum kit was purchased. Randy later credits Luchetti with giving him the guidance to help him realise his rock dreams.

A year later, Randy plays in his next band called Doc Rand and The Purple Blues with a black singer that can dance like James Brown. Wearing sparkly shirts and ties, they play a mixture of original tunes and covers, learning every track on James Brown's Live at the Apollo album. They soon beat The Sheltons in a battle of the bands competition at West Mesa High School, while James Brown and The Famous Flames is the first big concert that Randy sees.

The Purple Blues record a 7" single called I Need A Woman, which soon reaches number one on local radio station KQUO's weekly Top 40 chart and holds the spot for five weeks, turning Randy into a local star.

While attending West Mesa High School, Randy regularly plays until 1:30-2am with popular local band The Checkers, as his parents take turns sitting in the bars as chaperones and helping him to load his drum kit into their truck after the shows. This causes Randy to often fall asleep in class, but he really wants to be a musician more than anything in life.

As a senior, Randy plays in a symphonic band at the now-defunct University of Albuquerque and is named in the All-State symphonic band. He is recruited to attend school on scholarship, but after a year of school he decides he has had enough of the class room.

Randy plays in a band called The Tabbs when he is eighteen years of age and they wear mustard coloured Nehru jackets on stage. On 18 June 1970 he sneaks into a Jimi Hendrix concert and hides under the stage to get a closer look, exactly three months before Hendrix dies. He then plays with The Mudd after leaving The Tabbs and he begins experimenting heavily with drugs, including mescaline, peyote and heroin. The band's lead singer Tommy G dies of kidney failure, which Randy blames on Tommy's addiction to heroin. This causes him to shy away from using the drug again.

Rock Beginnings

He joins his first rock band in the late '70s called The Wumblies (originally called Cottonmouth) and he moves to Espanola where they predominantly play covers of songs by Yes, Black Sabbath, Led Zeppelin and Jethro Tull at as many gigs as possible, including high school proms. He first experiences life on the road with The Wumblies as they tour around America, playing four 45-minute sets a night in clubs. The band moves to Denver, Colorado where they fall apart in 1980; a year after his father Frank passes away at age fifty one.

Realising he has to move to Los Angeles if he wants to make it big, he makes the transition in 1981 with Albuquerque-bred guitarist Tim Pierce and they rent a run-down room together in Hollywood at the Montecito on Franklin Ave. Having endured enough of the local hookers and transvestites, they move out and Randy lives in his pickup truck. On the recommendation of another former Albuquerque musician, singer/songwriter Michael Goodroe, he joins pop band The Motels (whom Goodroe plays bass for) when their drummer falls sick with a heart condition just as they are about to go on tour. Randy embarks on his first major arena tour with The Motels in support of The Cars.

1951, MAY 4

MICK MARS

Robert (Bob) Alan Deal is born in Huntington, Indiana, USA on this Friday. He is born the second son of Tena Deal and Frank Deal, a factory foreman who suddenly one day becomes a Baptist minister. His older brother is Frank Jr. who later becomes a highway patrolman. His other siblings are brothers Tim and Randy, along with sister Susan.

Bob uses the alias Mick Mars from 1980, consistently saying over the years that the reason for the change was because he was never comfortable with his name, due to his initials spelling B.A.D. He tells the press he always liked the name Mick and chose Mars because of the Roman God of War.

Childhood

Bob comes down with scarlet fever at three years of age, and runs a temperature of 106 degrees for three days. He is so sick he nearly dies, and doctors later say he has possibly never recovered from it.

One day when five years of age, Bob and his younger brother Tim hang his older brother Frank from a tree with some baling rope, as they play Cowboys and Indians. His mum's sister Thelma, who lives at his grandmother's, pulls the noose from his neck after a short while; Frank is OK. The next week, Thelma takes the three boys to 4-H Fair in Hiers Park where Bob sees a man in a bright orange cowboy suit covered in rhinestones and wearing a big white Stetson hat introduce himself as Skeeter Bond to the crowd before singing. Seeing this first concert, young Bob knows that he wants to make music on stage, as his life.

That Christmas, he instantly chooses the stocking he sees with a tiny plastic guitar sticking out the top of it. The next Christmas his mother buys him a Mickey Mouse guitar, but he isn't interested in playing Mousketeer songs, instead getting a feel for how to tighten the strings and put melodies together. A kid that lives nearby, who Bob nicknames Sundance, teaches him to play his first real song called My Dog Has Fleas, on his guitar called Blue Moon, before showing him how to pick melodies.

His eldest cousin buys him a Stellar Acoustic guitar for Christmas when he is 9 years old, after seeing it in a pawn shop for twelve dollars. He teaches himself to play, learning a Righteous Brothers tune called B Flat Blues first; the B-side of their Cocoa Joe single.

A baby sister Susan, nicknamed Bird, is born soon after. When she is born with a collapsed lung, his parents decide to give up the tough Indiana winters, and move to a more arid climate on the advice of doctors. Ten members of the Deal family then drive for three days to Garden Grove, California in a '59 Ford where they begin their new lives.

His father works at a factory where they make cardboard boxes for Fender, and a year later his mother buys him a forty-nine-dollar St. George Rodeo electric guitar with some money she makes on weekends by ironing clothes. After making his own amp and stereo from his little sister's record player, he is soon making his own version of the surf music sounds that are popular in California at the time.

Bob discovers The Beatles and practices singing and playing for a year before performing The Beatles song Money in front of his family. His eldest cousin laughs at his singing and Bob gets so embarrassed he never tries to sing lead again in his life.

Teen Years

At age fourteen, Bob joins his first band, a Beatles cover band called The Jades, and he plays bass before replacing their guitarist. His first-ever gig is at the American Legion Hall in

Westminster, California and he makes five dollars, which is spent on new strings.

Through a Samoan friend, Joe Abbey, he meets the Ruiz brothers, who lead a street gang called the Bosco Brothers. He goes to their house to borrow an amp and reverb pedal and together they form a band called Sounds Of Soul, with Tony Ruiz on guitar, Johnny Ruiz on bass and Paulie Ruiz on drums. They play at various underage clubs in Orange County.

Bob also goes to school in Orange County and does well up until third grade, even though he acts the class clown and gets into heaps of fights. He earns the class clown title by trading insults with his 5th Grade teacher, Mr. Washburn. He tends to question things and form his own opinions on topics, and also likes to save his writings and memoirs. His love of the guitar is clearly evident, and he is one of the best three players in his school.

Bob gets suspended from school, following an incident where he writes an essay about the song Pressed Rat and Warthog by Cream and gets an F grade for it. Upon his return, a substitute teacher kicks him out of class for writing guitar chord charts in his Science notebook. He threatens the teacher as he walks out of school for the last time. The police then pay him a visit at the garden shed he lives in, behind his parents' house.

At Christmas, Bob's Aunt Annie gives him a beaten up Les Paul that she bought for ninety eight dollars. The following May, an acquaintance gives him a '54 Fender Stratocaster. Bob soon grows tired of rival gangs coming to the Ruiz Brothers' house for fights and their singer Antone tells Bob of a blues band in Fresno that is looking for a guitarist.

So at seventeen, Bob heads to Fresno, expecting to earn money from gigs with the new blues band he is joining, but even though he teaches the all-black band everything he knows about rhythm and soul, he feels he is wasting time since they can't play well enough for him. He gets a job picking watermelons to earn some money for food instead, but he soon heads back home.

He lives in the shed with a friend Ron and together they often swallow fistfuls of mini-white cross-top pills that are essentially truckers' speed. He then progresses to taking a heavy painkiller called Seconal, which he washes down with gin until his doctor says he will die if he doesn't quit. After feeling it's time to move away from his family again, he moves in with some bikers in Orange County. He also starts to feel pain in his hips and other bones.

Rock Beginnings

Bob plays clubs in a band called Wahtoshi with fellow musicians Jim Cunningham and Mike Malone; the name thought to mean number one in Chinese. His friend Mike Collins brings his sixteen-year-old former girlfriend Sharon Copas to a party and she begins dating nineteen-year-old Bob. Sharon soon finds out she is pregnant and they ask Bob's parents what they should do. Bob's father tells him to be a man and do the right thing, so he immediately proposes to Sharon while she is in the bathroom. They take a drive out to Las Vegas where they get married on 3 January 1971 in a small white chapel. Sharon gets Bob a job in the industrial laundry where she works. Their son is born on 9 August 1971 and named Les Paul by Bob after his favourite guitar brand, before Sharon falls pregnant again soon. A daughter is born to Bob and Sharon on 4 September 1973 in Westminster, California and named Stormy, after the Classics IV song.

As a married young father of two, Bob feels his life has run off track, so he turns to God. He forms a gospel band for a short while and a friend of his father baptises him, before Bob realises the church is not his answer. At the laundry one afternoon, a tub swings and smashes into Bob's left hand. He panics that such an accident may mean he can never play guitar again. Wahtoshi replaces him while his hand heals and he tells Sharon that he will never work a day job again. That Christmas, Sharon gets sick of working three jobs to support the family and takes young Les and five-month-old Stormy and leaves him. Broke, Bob moves back into the garden shed behind his parents' house and it isn't long before he spends two nights in jail for not making his $200 per month child support payments.

Upon his return from jail, Aunt Thelma takes him to see a back specialist, where he learns he has a degenerative bone disease called Ankylosing Spondylitis. Not knowing of any other relatives with it, he is told he has an extremely rare form of the inherited disease that begins in teenage years. Although they expect it to stop in his mid-thirties, it never does, causing him to always have inflamed and stiff joints.

Bob and Mike Collins hang out together, hitching to nightclubs on weekends in search of bands to jam with. During the summer of '73 they see a band called Whitehorse from Ocean Beach, California at Pier 11 in Costa Mesa. They had been gigging extensively since forming in September '72 as Fat City. Bob hangs around them for six months, whenever they are in town, and practices with second guitarist David Day, who had relocated to Santa Ana from Ocean Beach. Bob becomes good friends with drummer Jack Valentine and second guitarist/keyboardist David Day, who had a falling out with original band leader and first lead guitarist Kevin Kohl. Bob is later introduced to bassist Harry Clay and lead singer Kenny Morse, who both continue to live in Ocean Beach. Prior to Whitehorse, Harry had been in a San Diego band Catseye with Kenny, and used to jam with drummer Stewart Copeland (later of The Police) when Catseye weren't gigging.

Harry comes up with the name Motley Croo late in 1972 but management prefers Whitehorse, named after the bottle of Scotch whiskey. The name Motley Croo is utilised whenever the band shops their original tunes for a recording contract, but to this day, there is a disagreement amongst original Whitehorse members as to whether the band actually ever played any live gigs under the name Motley Croo or not.

David slowly teaches Bob the Whitehorse songs while David's previous band-mate, Kim Sherman from the recording group Frantics, fills in as the second lead guitarist for the group during a ten-week tour of Colorado in the Fall of '73. Kim is also instrumental in teaching Bob many of the sixty songs in the Whitehorse repertoire. Bob officially joins the group on stage as lead guitarist in January 1974 at Mr. Lucky's in Denver Colorado, during another ten-week Colorado tour, when Kim finally leaves to return to Los Angeles where he plays session guitar for Flash Cadillac.

During the thirty-six hour marathon return drive to Los Angeles in March '74, the band's equipment truck blows its engine in the Barstow desert, while Bob is driving. Dejected by the catastrophic expense, the band struggles to regain momentum. Harry books an opening slot with JoJo Gunne in San Diego and the group migrates to Huntington Beach. Harry and Jack have a large apartment there with a garage where the band can rehearse. Jack constructs the world's first upside-down drum machine here. The band reaches peak momentum with this line-up playing approximately 280 gigs a year, with Jack utilising his upside-down drums at many gigs. Bob moves into the apartment in Huntington Beach with Jack and Harry, sleeping on the living room floor in a sleeping bag behind a sheet taped to the ceiling. Bob prefers this arrangement because the apartment is cleaner than his previous home, and he soon hooks up with new girlfriend Marcia Tucker.

Tension has been rising over musical direction for the group. The band has five 24-track masters recorded with David, Harry and Kenny being the principal songwriters. Jack and Bob want the group to move in a harder, more progressive rock direction. They idolise the group Gentle Giant from England, as well as Deep Purple, while David, Harry and Kenny write and sing more straight-ahead rock songs in the vein of Spiders from Mars, Mott the Hoople and even Bachman Turner Overdrive. Soon after dislocating his ankle while sliding into third base playing semi-pro baseball, Jack Valentine leaves the band over unsettled musical differences in the fall of '75.

Kenny brings in new drummer Steve Jackson and new guitarist Chris Noe as Bob leaves the group for about six months. He helps Jack move to San Diego and soon moves in with him for a while. Jack gets him a job in a music store but he never shows up. They try to start a band with bassist Gary Chansley who had just left Wolfgang but Chansley accepts an offer to join San Diego's Peter Rabbit. They audition other bassists for a power trio but feel it is futile, so Bob moves back to Marcia in Los Angeles. While Bob is unemployed, Marcia falls pregnant. They struggle to survive on welfare as Marcia is unable to continue working as a cocktail waitress and part-time nurse due to the advancing pregnancy, and they become homeless, often living in her VW van. When Kenny leaves to join Holy Smoke, which later evolves into Vendetta, Bob rejoins Whitehorse with Harry and David. Bob, Harry and David move into the former Flash Cadillac mansion on Wilton Boulevard in Hollywood during the summer of '76. With new vocalist Buzz Hatton and drummer Bill Forbes, they again pick up momentum.

A son, Erik Michael Deal, is then born in Cedar Sinai Hospital to Bob and Marcia on 18 August 1976. With the five band members, girlfriends, baby Erik Deal, two roadies, former guitarist Kim Sherman, and Buffalo Springfield drummer Dewey Martin all living in the three-storey dilapidated Victorian, the house defines insanity.

Despite the fact that Whitehorse gig constantly with all members making equal money, Bob is very poor at managing his finances and has to sell out his shares in the Whitehorse truck and equipment, as well as often requiring cash advances to stay afloat. When Buzz Hatton departs as the band's vocalist in the summer of '77, Micki Marz (Michelle Meyers) joins after walking on stage to audition live during a gig at Gazarri's. Whitehorse finally breaks up in December 1977 when another band from England releases an album that is reviewed in Rolling Stone magazine as "So-California's Whitehorse", while the real Whitehorse has three new 24-track tunes in the can and several offers pending from major labels. When they take legal action, the band's lawyers negotiate a $20,000 settlement with Whitehorse to resume under the name Motley Croo but the new drummer Mike Tolan, Micki and Bob push for $100,000, which blows negotiations out of the water, and they end up with nothing, except the end of their band.

Bob then decides to keep playing Top 40 with David Day from Whitehorse in Ten-Wheel Drive, while Harry Clay starts an original outfit in 1978 called Video Nu-R with former Shady Lady singer Stefan Shady, before he's replaced on vocals by Randy Lee Miller. Once Video Nu-R begin to gig steadily at the Starwood and other Hollywood clubs Bob joins them on guitar, as he, Marcia and young Erik continue to live with Harry and David in the Whitehorse house. Harry works at Betnun Music in Hollywood and finances the recording and pressing of Video Nu-R's two 7" singles; the first titled Gypsy Woman/You Drive Me Crazy in December 1978, followed by Decadence Plus in September 1979. This is Bob Deal's first record to be released and both singles receive limited radio airplay in Los Angeles on both KNAC and KMET but Harry finds it increasingly difficult to support the band financially.

During 1979, Harry, Bob, Marcia and Erik move to a new apartment and rehearsal studio on Magnolia Boulevard in North Hollywood but it's not long before Bob and Marcia split up as he doesn't want to marry her and she can not afford to buy young Erik his first pair of walking shoes. For the baby's sake and survival, she decides that she needs to move on, thus freeing Mick of the responsibility so he can focus on his music career and she can finish her schooling and find a better job to enable her to take care of their child on her own.

Bob's music career struggles again as Randy Lee Miller quits Video Nu-R after seeing beer bottles being hurled during their set at the Troubadour. Subsequent line-up changes alter the politics in the band and Bob is soon told he has to leave the band, just as they are about to go into the studio with Warner Brothers Records to record the Decadence Plus single. The record deal evaporated and everyone was upset within the band. The single ends up being recorded after the drummer scores one hour of free time at Mystic Sound in Hollywood, where they record the song live in one take with Bob Deal back on guitar, Harry Clay shouting rapid fire vocals over bass synth and organ, and a coked-out drummer playing too fast. With his time in Video Nu-R now at an end after recording his first music, Bob places an ad in The Recycler reading, "Extraterrestrial guitarist available for any other aliens that want to conquer the Earth" and he receives many bizarre calls. For a very short time, he bounces back to David Day's steady cover band Ten-Wheel Drive and their semi-resident gig at the Stone Pony, within walking distance down Magnolia.

Sheriffs come to the apartment looking for Bob due to non-payment of child support for his kids. Bob has no assets at all and no regular income, making it impossible to meet his payments. He finds work at a motorbike factory on Magnolia where he cleans carburetors, however the pain from his disease makes him a useless worker and it only lasts a few months.

He re-connects with original Whitehorse singer Kenny Morse in the middle of 1979 and soon joins his band, replacing guitarist Chris Noe, and they immediately change their name from Holy Smoke to Vendetta. Quickly leaving town to escape his legal problems, he moves into the band house in North Redondo Beach, once again in the living room and once again sleeping behind a sheet hung from the ceiling. With Kenny on vocals, Bob on guitar, Johnny Gall on keyboards, Barry Leab on bass and Steve Meade (aka Kinky McKool) on drums, their set consists of at least twenty originals along with hits by Foreigner, Led Zeppelin, The Cars and other heavy bands. Bob sings occasional background vocals during their sets, as well as lead vocals on the Elvis Costello song Pump It Up. Although he sounds good, he doesn't really have the confidence to carry it.

Bob has no vehicle and relies on his new best friend John 'Stick' Crouch for transport, who also helps the band as a driver and road crew whenever they travel. Vendetta plays rock clubs from L.A. to South Bay to San Diego to Yuma, keeping their licks up and avoiding the 'prissy, colourful silk/satin and scarves' look, opting for leathers and Levis instead. The Top 40 clubs don't hire them because of their look and attitude, so they end up playing the dives.

Bob really starts to come into his own as a guitarist but is still always broke and needs money to catch up on child support. Vendetta travels to Alaska at the end of October for some higher paying gigs, as disco has not caught on and phased out rock bands up there. Two American mercenaries fresh from El Salvador hang out with the band, liking them so much that they drive around Anchorage and literally shoot out the marquees of other clubs.

Hating his real name and hoping to avoid arrest for his mounting debt, Bob Deal changes his name while in Alaska. When Vendetta flies back to California on 1 January 1980, Bob is now Mick Mars. His new name is very similar to that of former Whitehorse front woman, Micki Marz. He buys another Les Paul and Marshall stack with his gig money upon return.

When at home in the South Bay area, a lot of their friends and acquaintances – like Don Dokken, Juan Croucier and Bobby Blotzer – come by to catch Vendetta performances. Once in a while, they see actor Robin Williams sitting in the back of Pier 52 playing harp along to their songs. Another night at Pier 52, blues singer Big Mama Thornton stumbles in and joins the band on stage for Hound Dog – the song she wrote back in 1953 and made even more famous by Elvis Presley three years later.

Singer Kenny Morse quits Vendetta in the fall of 1980 and the band tries to continue on for a few months. Mick's loyal friend Stick tries to get his brother-in-law Allan Coffman to back Vendetta financially but they are falling apart. So with Vendetta splitting and needing cash, Mick again plays covers at the Stone Pony with his former Whitehorse band-mate David Day in Ten-Wheel Drive, who changes name to Spiders and Cowboys.

One night before a gig late in 1980, Mick walks into Magnolia Liquor Market on Magnolia Boulevard in Burbank to get a half-pint of cheap tequila. Behind the counter he meets Frank Feranna (about the same time that he becomes Nikki Sixx) and they chat about bands they are into; none of which are the same. He invites Frank to come down the road and see him play later that night at the Stone Pony in Spiders and Cowboys. They get drunk together after Mick's set where he plays slide guitar with the mike stand. At the end of the show he gives Frank his phone number.

1958, DECEMBER 11

NIKKI SIXX

Franklin Carlton Serafino Feranna's life begins in San Jose, California, USA at 7:11am on this Thursday morning. His nineteen-year-old mother, Deanna Lee Haight (born 5 May 1939), an attractive and wildly adventurous farm girl from Idaho, wants to name him Michael or Russell, but the nurse asks his Sicilian father, Frank Serafino Feranna (born 8 April 1918), who immediately names him after himself. When Nikki is ten months old, his mother splits from his father and moves to live with his "Nona" Emma Ervina Poe and her second husband, Tom Reese, whom she married when Deanna was sixteen.

A couple of months later, his alcoholic parents have a girl named Lisa Marie. Not growing up around him, his mother later tells him that Lisa left home not wanting anyone to contact her. However, he finds out during 1997 that she has a very acute case of Down's syndrome and is blind, mute and unable to walk. Nikki sees her for the first time at her funeral in 2000.

Later in life, Frank learns that his father had a son named Randy with another woman, eight years before he was born.

Childhood

Frank and his mother, who dates actor Richard Pryor for some time, live on the ninth floor of the Sunset Towers on Sunset Boulevard. Young Frank often spends a lot of time with his mother's parents, who threaten to take legal custody of Frank if his mother doesn't give up her party hard ways.

When Frank is four, his mother dates then marries Bernie Comer, the trumpet player in Frank Sinatra's backing band, in which she herself is singing backup vocals. They live in a little brown house in Lake Tahoe, where Bernie is abusive to him. A few Christmases later, a sister Ceci is born, and Frank's birth father visits, giving him a red plastic sled with leather handles. Planning on getting married again to a woman who can't have kids, Frank's father wants to see what kind of kid Frank is, to see if he is worth taking.

At six years of age, they move to Mexico, where Frank has the most enjoyable period of his childhood. His mother and Ceci fly there, while he rides with Bernie in a drive across the border in a Corvair, with Bernie's German Shepherd dog named Belle that frequently bites Frank. He smokes marijuana for the first time, with his mother at seven years of age.

He soon moves to live with his grandparents in Idaho, where he often encourages his cousins to sing along with him as they play. He calls his grandmother Nona. El Paso, Texas is the destination of his next relocation, where his grandfather, Tom Reese, works at a Shell gas station and they live in a trailer. He's a fast learning and intelligent child, which causes him to get bored in school.

They then move to a ranch in Anthony, New Mexico for a year, where his grandparents hope to make money with a hog farm. One day he slices his finger on the pigpen so bad that it is hardly attached, wobbling and shooting blood. Another day while living there, he gets struck by lightning in a doorway. One of Frank's chores is to slaughter the rabbits that they also raise. He takes an interest in words around the age of nine or ten, writing poetry and little stories. He gets bullied on the school bus, until he learns how to stand up for himself by retaliating with violence, which helps kick start his juvenile delinquency.

The farm doesn't work out for his grandparents, so they move back to El Paso where he attends Gasden District Junior High. He begins stealing from lockers and the general store called Piggly Wiggly's. He slashes tyres with a buck knife he was given for Christmas by his grandfather, who sold his radio and only suit to afford it.

After moving back to a sixty-acre cornfield in Twin Falls, Idaho at eleven years of age, Frank takes up football, which he uses as a release to counter his aggression from being picked on. He starts taking notice of girls, and one day hears the song Big Bad John by Jimmy Dean on the radio, and requests it until he's told to stop calling the station.

Teen Years

He moves with his grandparents again – this time to Jerome, Idaho, where he eventually buys his first album. He saves enough to buy Deep Purple's Fireball but finds himself buying Nilsson Schmilsson by Harry Nilsson at the suggestion of his friend's sister, with whom Frank is infatuated. The first live band he sees is at the high school gym in Jerome with about three hundred kids of the town's population of three thousand. Frank's first sexual encounters are with a girl named Sarah Hopper and he gets laid for the first time at thirteen, in the back of her parents' car, while they're in church.

He becomes too difficult for his grandparents to look after, so he moves to Seattle to live with his mother and sister Ceci, with the hope of improvement in his attitude and actions. They live in the Queen Anne Hill area with his mother's new Mexican husband Ramone, who listens to a lot of Hispanic jazz and funk, and tries to teach Frank how to play guitar on a battered old acoustic.

They then move to welfare apartments nearby in Fort Bliss. At his new school, Frank befriends a rocker, Rick Van Zandt, who soon says he needs a bass player for his band. So at age fourteen, he steals his first guitar (thinking it was a bass) from a music store called Music West that he frequents daily between bus trips to school. He asks for an application for work and stuffs the guitar into an empty guitar case he had loaned from a friend of Rick's. After the band tells him it is not a bass, he sells it and buys a black Rickenbacker bass with a white pick guard and tries to learn by listening to The Stooges and Aerosmith songs, but they realise he can't play. Frank jams with a guy over the road, as he is starting a band called Mary Jane's, but he's hopeless. He tries his hand jamming with various other bands, some called Forced Entry and Sleaze.

After befriending a punk rocker, Gaylord, who has his own apartment and a band called The Vidiots, he becomes part of a circle of friends that are called The Whizz Kids, due to their glammed-out appearance. Doing a lot of drugs, Frank practically moves into the apartment and sells drugs for them. He gets into fights at school as kids call him Alice Bowie, and he breaks into houses on the way home, stealing whatever he can.

After an argument with his mother in which he throws his stereo and destroys the TV, he asks for a knife from a nearby house, and proceeds to stab himself above the elbow deep to the bone. He calls the police and tells them that his mother attacked him, so they will arrest her and take her away. Instead, the police say if he presses charges he will have to live in a juvenile home for four years until he turns eighteen. He drops the charges and leaves home, sleeping at a friend's house until he is kicked out, before turning to Rick Van Zandt's parents' car for his bed. Frank is eventually thrown out of Roosevelt High School after another couple of months; expelled for selling joints, at his seventh school in eleven years – thus ending his school education.

Frank then gets a dishwashing job at Victoria Station and shares the rent for a one-bedroom apartment with seven others, until he quits the job and is forced to move out. He then sleeps in the closet of two prostitutes who feel sorry for him, until he has to move out, going back to his friend's car. He sells his bass so he can buy drugs to peddle for more money.

At seventeen, he gets busted selling chocolate-coated mescaline outside a Rolling Stones concert at the Seattle Coliseum to survive. After being threatened with a ten-year minimum jail sentence, he is let free and decides he needs to leave the city and try to get his life on track.

After calling his mother, she puts him on a Greyhound bus the following day. With his Aerosmith tape, a Lynyrd Skynyrd tape and a beaten up player, he heads back to his grandparents' farm in Jerome, Idaho. He works hard, moving irrigation pipes to earn money and soon buys a $109 replica Gibson Les Paul from a gun shop.

One day his mum's sister Sharon visits with her husband Don Zimmerman, who is president of Capitol Records in Los Angeles. Don starts to send him packages of magazines and cassette tapes of bands such as the Sweet and The Beatles, with Frank particularly liking heavier songs like Back in the USSR and Helter Skelter.

Rock Beginnings

He saves up a bus fare to Los Angeles, where he initially stays with his Aunt Sharon and Uncle Don for four or five months. Don gets him a job at a record store called Music Plus and lets him drive his Ford pickup, but arrogant and ungrateful Frank is soon kicked out to be on his own again. He takes a one-bedroom apartment near Melrose Avenue and manages to not pay any rent for eighteen months, before the police finally evict him. He buys a run down '49 Plymouth for one hundred dollars and dates a girl named Kaitie. It's not long before he's getting fired from the record store for stealing from the till; he punches the one-armed owner when confronted.

Frank then gains work as a telemarketer, selling Kirby vacuum cleaners, until he takes a carpet steam-cleaning job, stealing whatever he can from inside client homes. He puts together his first band named Rex Blade, with a hairdresser Ron on vocals who lived with him for a while, a girl named Rex and her boyfriend Blake. They rehearse in an office building next door to punk band The Mau-Maus, before Frank is kicked out of the band.

Finding a garage in the classifieds for a hundred dollars per month, Frank sleeps on its floor with his only possessions: his stereo and mirror. Intent on buying some decent music equipment, he works from 6am to 6pm dipping computer circuit boards into chemicals at a Woodland Hills factory, before starting a 7pm to 2am shift at Magnolia Liquor Market in Burbank, where he steals as much alcohol as possible while also cheating the till. It's here that he first meets Mick Mars one night. He goes to many auditions for bands, as he tries to find others with a passion for Johnny Thunders, Slade, Kiss and the Sweet.

Early in 1979, he answers another ad and hooks up with guitarist Lizzie Grey (real name Steve Perry), with whom he joins his first real band with, called Sister. The band was put together in 1976 by Blackie Lawless, and has Chris Holmes on guitar (who both later form W.A.S.P.), but Sister disbanded. Blackie has also spent a small amount of time in the New York Dolls after replacing Johnny Thunders for a few months, before moving to Los Angeles and forming Killer Kane prior to Sister, when the New York Dolls fell apart. Trying to revive Sister, they rehearse on Gower St in Hollywood, but with their pentagrams and worm-eating antics, they never make it onto the stage with this new lineup featuring Frank and Lizzie. After three days in a little recording studio in South Bay trying to record an album, they decide the sessions are terrible and they scrap the whole idea. Frank is kicked out and when Lizzie follows suit the pair decide to form their own band.

He soon moves into a place in Beachwood Canyon with his singer girlfriend Angie Saxon (real name Annette Diehl), who works as a secretary and rehearses with her band. She kicks him out after he tries to sleep with her roommate, and Frank finds himself living in a Hollywood slum and hanging out in famed local rock clubs like the Whisky A Go-Go, the Roxy Theatre, the Rainbow Bar and Grill, and the Starwood, as he tries to get his band going.

Frank and Lizzie put together a new band called London, with a drummer named Dane Rage, keyboardist John St. John, and Michael White on vocals, who is later fired and feels Frank is too concerned with image. White is replaced with former Mott The Hoople vocalist Nigel Benjamin (he replaced Ian Hunter in Mott), who answers their ad in The Recycler. Frank is ecstatic and sends some photos of London to his idol – Brian Connolly from the Sweet – after having his Uncle Don hook him up, but Connolly basically tells him to keep his day job. This further inspires Frank.

After being fired from his current two jobs doing more telephone sales and selling light bulbs, Frank works when he feels like it at Wherehouse Music in Hollywood, and sometimes donates blood at a clinic for money. Still broke, he manages to contact his father in San Jose who completely rejects him, pretending he doesn't have a son. He doesn't see him again before he dies in Santa Clara on 27 December 1978, when he has a heart attack in his shower.

While living in North Hollywood, he dates The Orchids' drummer Laurie Bell (real name Laurie Milmerstadt), after meeting her through Kim Fowley of The Runaways. The Orchids are an all-female band formed from the ashes of The Runaways. On 14 August 1980, Frank signs a music publishing agreement with Kim Fowley's Rare Magnetism Music for the publishing rights and royalties to a song Stop Hanging On to Yesterday that he co-writes with Laurie.

He kills Frank Feranna Jnr. in the lyrics to a new song On With the Show before lodging a Decree Changing Name form on 7 November 1980 in the Superior Court of California as he becomes Nikki Sixx. He started using the name a few months ago, after recalling the time he was looking through a scrapbook with his former girlfriend Angie, which included photos she had taken of a Southern Californian band called Squeeze with a guy called Niki Syxx (real name Jeff Nicholson). Frank was fascinated by the name and asked what he was up to now; Angie said he was in the surf band Jon & The Nightriders. Thinking it was a cool name, Nikki Sixx became Frank's new identity.

In later years, Nikki tells the media the name was inspired by the first two characters on his Californian driver's license: N6. Jeff Nicholson actually came up with the name by first calling himself Niki Olson as derived from his surname. Still uncomfortable, he kept the first name Niki as he thought about a new surname. Driving in Newport Beach one day in 1975, he pulled behind a Mercedes Benz with license plates NIKI 6, so he decided to call himself Niki Syxx from then on. He soon dated a girl named Beth Salvatore, who asked him how he got his name. It turned out that it was her mother's Mercedes – Niki was her mum's first name and the number 6 represented the number of people in their family.

London is managed by David Forest, who owns the Starwood where they often play, and Nikki and Dane also work there as cleaners. This club becomes a home of sorts, as Nikki is introduced to celebrities and stronger drugs. One night Mick Jagger and Keith Richards come to see London play at the club. Nikki writes a song called Public Enemy #1 with Lizzie in his '74 Ford Pinto, while they drink rum and Coke.

After rising to the top of the Los Angeles club circuit with their brand of originals, and a few David Bowie and Mott The Hoople covers, London is unable to secure a recording contract with their demo. Singer Nigel Benjamin quits London, as musical differences become prevalent and the band falls apart. Nikki has co-written about half of the band's original tunes but he keeps some others aside for his other musical ideas and aspirations.

1959, April 26

John Corabi

John Corabi is born in Philadelphia, Pennsylvania, USA on this Sunday. He's raised by his two conservative parents of Italian descent. After being the first born, he is followed by sisters Anna and Janet, then brothers Nicholas and Todd.

One day when he is nine years of age, his Mum points out The Beatles to him on TV and he thinks they are awesome. He then gets a Sears and Roebuck guitar for his first instrument. One of the first concerts he attends is the KISS Alive tour in the mid-'70s. John plays with many different bands throughout his high school teen years. His main influences are Aerosmith, Led Zeppelin, The Beatles, Humble Pie and Deep Purple.

Struggling in his early days as a musician, John works as a telemarketer selling inflatable boats and toner for photocopiers. He also works numerous other jobs, where he drives cars, makes pizzas and sandwiches, as well as spending some time working in construction.

John dates a girl named Valerie at eighteen years of age, who is the sister of one of the members of his cover band at the time. Valerie has a young daughter and in two more years, they marry and then have their own son named Ian Karac Corabi in 1987.

1961, FEBRUARY 8

VINCE NEIL

Vince Neil Wharton is born in the Queen of Angels Hospital, Hollywood, California, USA on this Wednesday. He later lops his surname to be known as Vince Neil.

Standing at more than six-feet-tall, his half-Native American father Clois Odell Wharton, but known as Odie, is an auto mechanic who works as a Maintenance Supervisor of sheriff's cars for the LA County Mechanical Division. Odie was born in a one-room farmhouse shack in the rural outskirts of Paris, Texas to his mother from Tupelo, Mississippi, and father who was orphaned in Oklahoma at a young age when his part-American Indian parents died. Odie moves with his parents and sister to California in 1941 when he is five years old, and his father paints houses for a living. As a member of the Shifters car club, Odie meets his future wife Shirley one night at the drive-in. They date for a while during high school, until he quits school and joins the army in 1956, where he serves in Germany for a couple of years between the Korean and Vietnam wars.

Vince's half-Spanish mother, Shirley (nee Ortiz), grew up in Albuquerque, New Mexico as one of five children, before they move to the Inglewood district in southwestern Los Angeles. Her machinist father dies at forty-two when she is young, and they then move to the Watts neighbourhood. After graduating, Shirley becomes a hairstylist and goes to cosmetology school in Hollywood. She later works nights at a Max Factor factory, packaging lipsticks and makeup products for shipping country-wide. She also loves listening to Motown soul music. Shirley marries Odie on 22 November 1958 in Las Vegas, and gives birth to a sister for Vince when he is sixteen months old.

Childhood

Four-year-old Vince witnesses the Watts Rebellion – a riotous racial uprising triggered by police brutality in his grandmother's neighbourhood, which sees thirty four people die, just over a thousand get injured, as $40 million of property damage caused. Vince watches some of the four-thousand-strong California Army National Guard who help suppress the disturbance, and is fascinated by the troops.

Vince's parents move to 1836 E Dimondale Drive in Compton, near the oil refineries. At the time it is a nice, new neighbourhood with lots of blue-collar working people and affordable for the middle-class, but it soon changes to a predominantly black and lower class district rife with gang activity. When they reach elementary school, they are the only white students in attendance.

Vince goes to a music shop with his dad one day, who buys him his first guitar. He takes some regular lessons up to the age of ten, but never really feels comfortable playing it, so he prefers to strut around in his bedroom miming to Aerosmith songs like Walk This Way and Rod Stewart's Hot Legs. Vince enjoys playing Little League baseball for the Dodgers in Carson. He also takes tap dance and ballet lessons, and is very good at figure skating on ice after being inspired to learn when watching his sister perform.

One night as the family is playing a board game, a bullet comes through his sister's window at the front of the house, as a result of feuding from local rival gangs The Crips and the AC Deuceys; a rental Crips clubhouse is directly across the road. On another occasion on the way home from Broadacres Avenue Elementary School at about ten years of age, Vince witnesses the shooting of a teenager as four kids steal his sneakers. A few days after the incident, the same kids come out of the Crips house across the road and approach Vince as he waits for the ice cream van outside his home in broad daylight. The tallest of them grabs him, turns him around and takes the fifteen cents from his pockets that he was going to use for his ice cream. Vince then feels a pressure across his throat, and when he feels wetness, he realizes he's been sliced under his chin from ear to ear with a blade, missing his jugular vein by an inch.

After spending the night at hospital where he is stitched up, his teacher, former Playboy Playmate Mrs. Anderson, allows him to hold her hand as they walk into class the next day. Vince takes every opportunity to get close to her and credits her with opening up his first sexual feelings. The following year he finds himself sticking his hands up the skirt of a neighbourhood girl Tina under a doghouse.

To survive the tough neighbourhood, Vince makes friends with bigger kids and becomes accepted as cool, but soon turns to delinquency as well. He would throw rocks at cars driving down the street, and once got caught when chased. He often plays with BB guns and sets fire to rubbish bins at school.

After school one day in sixth grade, he steals a backpack full of giant conch shells, coral necklaces and sponges from a warehouse full of souvenirs with three black kids and a Samoan. He buys his first cassette, Cloud Nine by The Temptations, with the money he makes from selling the stolen seaside items at the Compton swap meet. He loves to listen to the soul music of The Four Tops, The Spinners, and Al Green on the radio. With his five-dollar weekly allowance for washing the car and doing other chores, he buys 7" vinyl singles of 1972-74 pop songs like Smoke On The Water by Deep Purple, Dream On by Aerosmith, Hooked On A Feeling covered by Blue Suede, The Night Chicago Died by Paper Lace, and Clap For The Wolfman by The Guess Who.

Teen Years

Caught running out of a warehouse with a box full of stolen garden supplies, Vince is handcuffed and driven home in the back of a police squad car. His parents decide to send him and his sister to his Aunt's house in West Covina, to quickly escape the tough suburb until they can sell their home and secure another at 1551 Bruning Ave, Glendora. His mum then works in dental brace factory Ormco and transfers Vince to Sunflower Junior High for seventh grade, where he struggles with school and discovers he has a form of dyslexia, which makes reading hard. He prefers to wag school a lot of the time and go surfing at Seal Beach and Huntington Beach, instead of working harder at his education. He loves listening to The Beatles' white album, and enjoys his time playing in a flag football team. Walking to school one day, he finds a sex manual paperback book, which he stashes inside his neighbour's shed. He rips out the pictures and sells them to school kids for a quarter each. After selling about seventy pages, the gym coach finds some in a locker and the kids rat him out, so Vince gets suspended from school.

Even though he doesn't have a driver's license at age fifteen, his father buys him a primer brown '53 Chevrolet 3100 pick-up for $700, thinking his friend who untruthfully says he has a license could drive them to Charter Oak High School in Covina. Vince does a lot of work on the truck, including re-doing the inside button-tuck leather upholstery, adding an orange sunset mural on the tailgate, and adding surfboard racks across the truck's rear bed. The vehicle also gives him free reign to spend more time at the beach, where he also explores with drugs, alcohol and sex.

The first time he takes drugs is when he smokes a joint or two with girlfriend Penny Panknin at her house. The second time is at drive-in while watching the movie Silver Streak with four friends in a '65 Nova, when his surf mate John Marshall hands him a pipe of marijuana laced with angel dust. Before long he smokes angel dust in English class with a pipe that looks like a pen to prevent being caught, but when he is busted and sent to the principal's office, he is found wandering lost around a football field a couple of hours later. John also introduces him to white cross-top pills that he combines with angel dust, making him aggressive.

During a school lunchtime in his freshman year, he finds his stolen surfboard racks in the car of known bully and football player named Horace. When Vince confronts him about the theft, he denies it, so Vince punches him, breaking his nose and cheekbone before getting knocked unconscious as his head hits the floor. This shocks his football friends watching on before an ambulance is called. Ten minutes into class, the principal drags Vince out and has him charged with assault by the police. Although the charges are dropped at the station, he is suspended from school for two weeks, but is respected and treated like a hero upon his return. Horace's parents sue the Whartons and Vince's dad goes to court and pays them about $500.

Rock Beginnings

Vince and his friend John try to pick up girls at the Roller City skating rink near school. Here they often participate in a daily lip-synching contest, dressing up in flares, polyester shirts and wigs, to perform Let It Ride by Bachman Turner Overdrive. Winning his first contest, Vince realises he loves to perform on stage and it's further confirmed when he gets laid afterwards. After two weeks of driving to contests on the circuit, he wins again when performing You Really Got Me by The Kinks. Surprisingly, he sings it out loud himself, instead of lip-synching. In July 1978, Vince sells t-shirts outside Long Beach Arena as Van Halen performs a concert there on their first world tour, and he fanaticises about what it would be like to perform on such a big stage with a real band.

Growing in confidence, Vince drives girls home for sex during school lunch breaks while his parents are at work. One lunch break, he makes love to a girl Tami Jones in his pick-up truck in the car park. A year older than him, he had met Tami at a skating pipeline in Glendora after he had broken his leg. After not thinking any more of it and enjoying being with other girls, two months later Tami tells him she wants to follow through with her pregnancy to him. Vince tries to do the right thing and make a go of it, spending a lot of time with her – Tami even moves into his family's home for a while – and he supports her best he can when she is kicked out of school for pregnancy. At age seventeen, Vince's first child Neil Jason Wharton is born on

3 October 1978, as it's said Vince is working as a roadie loading sound equipment for a concert by The Runaways. He is the only student at school paying child support, but the young couple is also helped with the raising of Neil by their parents.

A guitarist James Alverson transfers to Charter Oak High School and soon asks Vince to be in his band since he has the longest hair in the school – he preferred to keep his locks instead of joining the school varsity baseball team when the coach says he would have to cut it. Vince goes with Tami to meet James in Charter Oak Park next to school and shows him his cheap guitar. When James asks if he can sing, Vince says he sung in a band called Black Diamond, and James correctly thinks he's lying. Vince's dad buys him his first microphone and they get together at a house in Hacienda Heights belonging to a friend of James' from his previous school in East Los Angeles – Nicaraguan bass player Danny Monge. Their Charter Oak classmate drummer Robert Stokes is also brought in to jam. As they play Hot Legs by Rod Stewart, James quickly realises Vince hasn't really sung before, but sees his potential. They rehearse more in Vince's garage, and then in the living room of Tami's sister. Danny is quickly replaced on bass by Greg Meeder from Glendora High for a while, before their roadie friend Joe Marks from Charter Oak High eventually takes over. James comes up with the band name Rockandi, after the Montrose song Rock Candy, but written differently. Since they are under the age required to play bars, they plan to play as many backyard parties as they can. Covers of I Want You To Want Me by Cheap Trick, Sweet Emotion by Aerosmith and Smokin' In The Boys Room by Brownsville Station are played at their first performance at their school during lunch break, while other songs by AC/DC, Led Zeppelin, ZZ Top, Pat Travers, Bad Company, Eddie Money, Black Sabbath, and The Sweet are soon worked on and added to their roster. Vince often sits in his truck and writes down the lyrics while listening to songs on eight-track tapes, as he mimics the singers' vocal styles. Rockandi quickly builds a reputation as the best party band in the area during 1978, after they coax unpopular students to host weekend parties while their parents are out to gain popularity and girls, and have the band perform while charging a dollar entry fee.

Vince organises a party at his own house one Friday night, advertising it on telephone poles around the city. Tami works as a door-girl, collecting a dollar entry fee at the back gate. His band sets up under the patio beside the pool and Vince performs in front of the 300-400 people in attendance. During the performance, Vince's parents return home from shooting some pool with friends nearby, and are shocked to see so many people there, under the impression from Vince that it was only going to be a small affair. Eventually the police arrive and disperse the party using megaphones.

He gets kicked out of Charter Oak High in 1978 for lack of attendance and begins cleaning at a recording studio and PA hire company in Covina in exchange for rehearsal time for his band. Realising he is going nowhere, he takes his parents' advice and enrolls in Royal Oak High in Covina for the start of his senior year. At school, he soon becomes friends with Tom Bass (later to be known as Tommy Lee) who plays with another band on the backyard party circuit called US 101. They often skip school together to jam on music in Tom's garage, and crank AC/DC's Highway to Hell in his van.

Vince drops out of school early in 1979 and moves out of home with his clothes in a beer carton. He sleeps in Tom's van, who soon gets expelled from school. Vince earns money as a pizza delivery boy, and then joins the carpenter's union with Joe Marks as apprentices with Kasler Corporation on a freeway overpass site doing concrete formwork. Making good money, he finances a blue Datsun 240Z and adds surfboard racks to it, as his Chevy pick-up is left broken down in his parent's drive. Vince and Joe soon find the construction work too hard, so they quit. His 240Z gets repossessed. He dates a girl called Leah Graham who has her own 240Z and begins an apprenticeship with her father Raleigh's company Graham Electric, for whom he digs ditches and helps wire buildings. Leah acts as

Rockandi's manager by booking them gigs at places like the Starwood and Gazzari's, and putting ads in the paper.

1962, October 3

Tommy Lee

Thomas Lee Bass is born in Athens, Greece on this Wednesday. He is the first child for his ex-Miss Greece 1957 mother, Vassilikki Papadimitriou (known as Boula) and army sergeant father David Lee Thomas Bass, who was born in St. Paul, Minnesota.

His parents met at Boula's parents place when her sister brought David along to a christening for one of her kids so he could see how the Greeks celebrate christenings. On army service stationed in Greece, David told Boula that first day that he wanted to marry her. He bought her a ring the next day and they married in four more days, once she ditched her boyfriend. Not speaking a word of each other's languages, they communicate by drawing pictures.

Boula had five miscarriages before giving birth to their first boy, who died within days of his birth. Boula then stayed in bed for the nine months of her next pregnancy before giving birth to Tommy. Exactly one month after Tommy is born they move to Thailand for a while before returning to Athens.

Childhood

The family moves from Athens to the Los Angeles suburb of Covina, at 252 N. Lyman St. His mum works as a part-time house cleaner for some families, and his father works as the shop superintendent for the L.A. County Road Department, running the department that maintains road repair trucks and tractors, after being trained in diesel mechanics in the army. When Tommy is two his sister is born and named Athena Louise after her mother's homeland that she misses so much.

Tommy begins banging on things as soon as he is old enough to reach into the cutlery drawer, and at three years of age he often arranges pots and pans on the kitchen floor, hitting them with spoons and knives. At Christmas after he turns four, Tommy is given his first drum kit; a paper kit with a blinking light on the bass drum, a miniature cowbell and a cymbal, which helps keep their kitchenware from being damaged.

He sticks with accordion lessons with his sister for about four years until the age of ten when he finally quits because he finds it too hard. He has a DaVinci electronic accordion that he plugs into an amp and distortion box and cranks Deep Purple's Smoke on the Water. However, the band that influences him most is Kiss.

He tries his hand at tap dancing and ballet classes after a teacher calls upon their door, but he quits when the boys at school tease him. He tries his hand with piano lessons but is bored by the repetition of learning about scales, beats and bars. So he hassles his parents to buy him a guitar he had seen in a pawnshop, which he loves to play loud to as many people as he can.

Teen Years

After watching a marching band during a football game, Tommy decides he wants a proper drum kit and his father gives him a snare for Christmas. He subsequently works after school and weekends to buy his own kit, which his father co-signs for. His father helps him deck out their double-garage with soundproofing materials so he can practice, while they park their car outside in the driveway. Tommy's school friends with guitars like to come over and jam on rock songs.

Tommy loses his virginity at thirteen to the girl next door and best friend of his sister Athena, who walks in on them during their act on the floor of the garage studio. She tells their parents, making it a bad first experience for Tommy.

At around fourteen years of age, he hangs out down the street with his friend and gets turned on to Led Zeppelin records from his friend's older brother. He then gets acquainted with Black Sabbath, Van Halen, Cheap Trick, Ted Nugent and Deep Purple.

At school, music, co-ed volleyball and graphic design (where he makes Budweiser and rock t-shirts) are his favourite subjects. Tommy is often grounded by his strict and protective father, as he wags subjects he dislikes to sneak home and play his drums. In Grade 10, Tommy and some friends burn the grade book of his teacher Mr. Walker, which ends up having him suspended from school. His music teacher, Mr. Dvorak, is his favourite as he always allows him into Room 505 to play the drums and recognises his natural talent.

Tommy graduates to South Hills High School. Electing not to take drum lessons, he keeps his playing in check by joining the school marching band, as well as a local drum corp. He teaches others how to twirl sticks and leads his troop to many competition victories. However, he is a thorn in the side of the senior drum captain Troy, who punches Tommy in the nose one day, sending him to the hospital where they unsuccessfully try to straighten it.

The first concert he sees is Ted Nugent supported by Pat Travers. He is amazed and inspired by Pat's drummer Tommy Aldridge.

Rock Beginnings

His parents sell their house, moving fifteen minutes away, and Tommy starts his sophomore year at Royal Oak High in the Covina / San Dimas district. He forms his first band, a blues cover band, which jams in his garage but doesn't make it onto any stage. He then moves on to form a cover band called US 101 (named after the freeway that bisects Los Angeles) with some guys that later resurface in the band Autograph. They play songs by Journey, Boston, Foghat and Styx amongst others, and their parents are very involved in helping. Tom, the band's guitarist, is a surfer that loves the Beach Boys, and the band's set is also heavily influenced by it. Tommy's first gig is under lights at an outdoor concert at Upland High School's football stadium, which five hundred or so people enjoy. The band plays many school dances and backyard parties, with his sister Athena operating the lights. Tommy's dad often helps lug his drum kit as a roadie, while Tommy sometimes lights his drumsticks on fire while playing.

His father co-signs on Tommy's first car; a baby-blue Chevy van with tinted teardrop windows, Center Line rims, a Grand Canyon mural painted on the side, and a padded bed in the back.

On his band's circuit, he meets a blonde-haired surfer named Vince Wharton, who he thinks is very cool and sees that the girls adore him, especially when he sings in his band Rockandi. He goes to Charter Oak High, down the road, but starts coming to Tommy's school when he gets kicked out. Tommy then gets kicked out of Royal Oak and commences continuation school, only to drop out in his senior year, before working as a house painter with his uncle to earn money. He lets Vince sleep in his van after he leaves home during high school. When his parents find out, they let Vince sleep on Tommy's bedroom floor until he finds another place to live.

In a year or so, at seventeen years of age, Tommy grows tired of playing cover songs and he joins an original band called Suite 19, after his Rams cheerleader girlfriend Vicki Frontiere tells him they are looking for a drummer. They are a powerful three-piece instrumental outfit, with Jon Kemp on bass and a guitarist named Greg Leon. The band rehearses in Tommy's garage and plays some shows, thanks to Jon's booking agent mother, including a gig at the Starwood, where he has previously seen Judas Priest play. Frank Feranna (Nikki Sixx) sees the performance at the Starwood. Tommy also sees Frank's local band London play and is in awe of their performance.

Suite 19 supports UFO, Y&T and Quiet Riot before falling apart when Greg Leon jumps at the chance to join Quiet Riot following Randy Rhoad's departure. Jon Kemp then accepts an offer from Leif Garrett's manager to try and shape him into becoming the next big teen idol, while the rebellious and aggressive Tommy Lee hooks up with guitarist Mike Cusik (real name Michael Britton) to join his band called Dealer. Glenn Bassett plays bass in the four-piece, with Mark Poynter on keyboards, who had most recently been in the very popular L.A. band Snow. Before auditioning for Dealer, Tommy and his new band-mates take magic mushrooms before jamming on the original tunes.

Dealer records six songs, which is Tommy's first experience in a recording studio. However, he is continuously late for Dealer rehearsals or doesn't show up at all. During one rehearsal that he does attend, he angrily punches a hole in the wall of the practice room at the parents' house of one of the band members. Tommy soon steals Mark's girlfriend, a big-boned blonde twenty-year-old girl named Lisa, who can spray a fountain when having an orgasm. She is Tommy's first real girlfriend and is later nicknamed Bullwinkle by Vince because he thinks she has a face like a moose.

One day Tommy takes Lisa to the photo studio of his friend Will Boyett and gets frisky after some drinks. He starts pulling Lisa's clothes off in front of the camera before Lisa gives the naked Tommy a blowjob. While he is naked he decides he wants to do a couple of solo poses that could be sent to Playgirl, so pictures are taken of him posing the way Burt Reynolds did. (Will eventually sends the pictures to Playgirl who agrees to publish them until Tommy's attorney, David Rudich, threatens to sue him and Playgirl, so they remain unpublished.)

When Mark finds out about the photos and what Tommy has done with Lisa, it ends their relationship. The rest of Dealer backs up Mark because of Tommy's previous behaviour and they kick him out of the band, having drummed with them for at least six months.

Tommy joins a band called Sapphire with Brad Parker on guitar and Joey Vera on bass. Tommy and Joey quit after six months or so, and they look for a new band.

1981

1/81

Nikki Sixx jams with guitarist Greg Leon from a band called Suite 19 after seeing him play at the Starwood one night. Trying to put another band together, Nikki recalls the drummer in Suite 19 also stood out, so Greg gives him the recommendation and phone number of his former drummer Tommy Lee. Greg Leon later plays in Dokken, and DuBrow, who changed their name to Quiet Riot. He also forms the Greg Leon Invasion and hires Joey Vera on bass, at Tommy's recommendation. He later sells the name Invasion to Vinnie Vincent after his days in Kiss.

In years to come, Saturday 17 January 1981 is considered to be the birth of Mötley Crüe, which is seemingly when Nikki decided to form the new band that soon becomes Mötley Crüe.

2/81

Nikki calls Tommy who can't believe it is actually him on the phone; the same Nikki as in his London poster on his wall. They arrange to meet at the corner of Burbank Boulevard and Lankershim Boulevard in North Hollywood at a Denny's coffee lounge for lunch where Tommy and his friend Joey Vera meet him. They then head to Nikki's place in North Hollywood where he plays Tommy some demo songs, who starts beating to them on his living room table. Tommy then sets up his kit permanently in the front room of his place after a couple of days, happy to be playing with Greg again. Nikki soon fires the dowdy Greg Leon and they find a guy to replace him named Robin, via an ad in The Recycler. (Decades later, an online site claims this guitarist was Robin Moore, which was a stage name of Jeff Gill.)

3/81

With his friend Stick, Mick Mars rents the old Whitehorse truck from former band-mate Harry Clay to get Spiders and Cowboy's gear to a gig at Bojangles Nightclub in Yuma,

Arizona. Mick gets angry when the club owner in Yuma demands he turn down the volume, so he pushes over his stack at the end of their set and quits, thus playing his last Top 40 cover gig.

Tommy and Nikki search for a crazy second guitarist to off-set the dowdy Robin when Tommy reads a classified ad that Mick Mars has placed in The Recycler newspaper reading, "LOUD rude aggressive lead guitarist sks working band, xlnt equip, record credit & vocal ability - call Mick" along with his phone number, placed after a brainstorm with his former Vendetta drummer Steve Meade. Wanting to play original music instead of covers with Spiders and Cowboys, Mick gets a call from Tommy inviting him to an audition. He has his best friend John 'Stick' Crouch drive him, his guitar and his Marshall amps, which stick out the trunk of his burgundy 1971 Mazda RX-3 coupe, to Nikki's North Hollywood house. Tommy opens the house door and thinks Mick looks like Cousin Itt from the Adams Family. Mick and Nikki talk; both of them don't remember having met in the liquor store, then drinking together after Mick's set at the Stone Pony months earlier. They show Mick the opening riff to a song called Stick To Your Guns that was written by Nikki on piano. He originally wrote it for Blondie in 1979 at the request of Kim Fowley, but the band rejected it, so he reworks it for his new band. They think Mick does a great job, so they head out to buy a gallon of Schnapps at Mick's suggestion. Upon return, the three of them jam for an hour on some more songs Nikki had written, including Talk Of The Town and Public Enemy #1. After a couple more rehearsals with their sissy rhythm guitarist Robin, Mick feels he is not the right guy, so Nikki and Tommy say if he wants to be a fully-fledged member, he has to fire him. Mick is given the job after saying to Robin that he is the only guitar player. Robin cries upon being told the news from Mick. Having used the same colour hair dye, Nice & Easy Permanent Blue Black, certainly helped Mick's chances.

With Mick now in the band, Nikki dyes Tommy's hair black to look like his and Mick's. Tommy is convinced by Nikki to get a tattoo, so they go to Sunset Strip Tattoo and he decides upon a design of his favourite cartoon character Mighty Mouse, drawn bursting through a bass drum with sticks in his hands by Kevin Brady.

Nikki, Tommy and Mick go to check out a rhythm guitarist James Alverson in Rockandi, a band playing predominantly Cheap Trick and Sweet covers at the Starwood. With Mick not feeling comfortable about a second guitarist, his attention turns to the singer clothed in white satin pants and a white t-shirt ripped up the sides and sewn together with lace, belting out a version of Cheap Trick's song He's A Whore. Tommy recognises him as Vince Neil from his school days Royal Oak High, so Mick corners him in the bathroom after the show and tells him he is great. Tommy calls him a "blonde-haired bitch" and gives him his phone number to ring about auditioning the next weekend. Vince is happy in his band but agrees, so he doesn't hurt Tommy's feelings.

Tommy soon drops off a tape of the songs to Vince at his house and pleads with him to audition, but Vince says he is unsure about changing bands and then fails to show up at the audition. Vince, who frequently binges on cocaine, listens to the tape but feels the nameless band is lame. Several different singers are then auditioned.

The best vocalist to audition is twenty-eight-year-old Odean Peterson. He practices the songs Tonight (from The Raspberries' 1973 album titled Side Three), plus originals Can't Stop The Music, Talk of the Town, and Public Enemy #1. Although he is a decent singer, in time Nikki takes a dislike to his vocal pitch and they find his white gloves to be an un-cool image but they stick with it for the time being.

In the latter half of the month, the un-named band makes their way into Crystal Sound Studios at 1014 Vine St, Hollywood with engineer Laura Livingston, to record a demo tape of Nikki's songs: Stick To Your Guns, Talk Of The Town, Public Enemy #1 and cover song Tonight. When the allocated studio time runs out, Tommy makes out with Laura upon

Nikki's suggestion, ensuring more studio time for them to finish the recordings.

Allan Coffman, the thirty-eight-year-old brother-in-law of Mick's driver friend Stick, is interested in investing in a band. He flies in from Lake Tahoe to meet the band members and they demolish five bottles of Schnapps together. Allan returns another day with his wife Barbara and their two daughters for the new band to perform a little showcase for them. He proposes that he promotes them initially on an eight-week basis. The construction company owner, member of the county board of zoning administration, and ex-Vietnam MP officer and policeman, promises a twenty-dollar-per-week allowance to each member and sets up Coffman & Coffman Productions in Grass Valley, California; the name suggested by his wife Barbara, who is a Grass Valley School District board member.

29/3/81
Odean Peterson formally signs with the band as the vocalist. However, he refuses to take off his white gloves to record clapping at the end of the last song being recorded, Toast Of The Town, formerly Talk Of The Town. With a phone call later to Nikki and Tommy from Mick, they decide Odean is not going to cut it as their singer, so he's fired. Mick says he wants the singer from Rockandi to be in the band, due to the way he wooed the females in the audience when they saw him perform.

30/3/81
Rockandi was to play a party in Hollywood on the weekend, but the guitarist and bass player didn't show up, leaving Vince in the lurch. Vince called his guitarist James who says he has cut his hair short and wants the band to become a new wave act, which infuriated Vince, so he quit and is kicking himself for not auditioning with Tommy. Luckily, Tommy calls Vince again, who says he washed his jeans that had his phone number in it, even though he knows where Tommy lives. He organises for Vince to come to SIR Rehearsal Studios to audition, where

Missing Persons rehearses next door (and are subsequently left padlocked in their studio.)

1/4/81

On this Wednesday April Fools' Day, Vince auditions for the band at SIR Rehearsal Studios, singing along best he can to their songs. Everything gels between the members and they agree with manager Allan Coffman in attendance that Vince is the right singer to join the band, so he is hired. Nikki starts to re-write one of his songs to suit Vince's voice more, titled Live Wire.

Vince is driven to and from his audition as a passenger in a Datsun 280Z driven by his blonde girlfriend Leah Graham, who is his boss's daughter, where he works as an electrician currently building a McDonalds in Balwin Park. He lives with her at 2040 S Buenos Aires Drive in Covina. A rich drug-addict, Leah bought Vince his first leather pants from North Beach Leathers (later seen on Mötley's first album cover) for five hundred dollars and got him hooked on injecting cocaine. With her appearance and manner she's instantly nicknamed Lovey by the other guys as she reminds them of Lovey Howell from Gilligan's Island, even though she has been nicknamed Punky for years.

5/4/81

Nikki hosts a casual Sunday BBQ at his North Hollywood home he shares with girlfriend Laurie Bell. With the opportunity to play the Starwood in a couple of weeks for their first shows, they now need to decide upon their band's name. XMAS has been their leading contender and 'working title' to date, while other names considered are Trouble, Bad Blood, Holiday, and Suicidal Tendencies, as the they try to come up with a name that is already a commonly known and used word or phrase. Mick says they look like a motley crew and suggests the name Mottley Cru, having jotted it down in 1976 when he was rehearsing in the living room where he lived with his band Whitehorse. Nikki likes it and scribbles down some variations, settling on the spelling Motley Crue. Mick's friend Stick suggests they add umlauts over the 'o' to give it a militant, aggressive German feel, which is further inspired by the Löwenbräu beer they are drinking at the time. Tommy likes "the clean German sound" of bands like Accept and Scorpions, so this concept sits comfortably with him. Nikki takes it a step further and adds umlauts over the 'u' as well. He asks their photographer friend Don Adkins Jr. his thoughts, and he agrees it looks cool, even though it's not grammatically correct. The band now has its name – Mötley Crüe.

7/4/81

The first Mötley Crüe photo shoot takes place with Don Adkins Jr. in his parents' house at 18936 Stefani Ave, Cerritos.

8/4/81

The four Mötley Crüe band members and Coffman & Coffman enter into an Exclusive Management Agreement after Allan Coffman's attorney, who also represents Supertramp on behalf of their band manager Dave Furano, draws up some contracts to commence the partnership. They sign it on the spot. The ten-page agreement details aspects such as the duration of the agreement, upfront loans, commissions and weekly allowances. Each band member receives an advance of $250 the following day. Mötley Crüe signs a ten-year management deal with Allan Coffman. John 'Stick' Crouch works for Allan as his production man and representative on the ground in Hollywood.

15/4/81

Axed singer Odean Peterson of 1400 S Hayworth Ave, Los Angeles files a lawsuit in the Small Claims Court of Los Angeles against Allan Coffman, claiming $1000 for services rendered to the group Mötley Crüe and costs incurred.

The band continues work in the studio around this time, re-recording their demo. They erase Odean's vocals from the 24-track master and replace it with Vince singing. Not really knowing the songs very well, Vince sings the lyrics from sheets of paper (and it has been said you can hear the paper rustling on the recordings.) He is also very nervous since it is his first time in a recording studio. Not knowing how to get their record finished, Mick's friend Harry Clay hooks them up with the same pressing plant and printing company that produced the two singles they released when they were in Video Nu-R a couple of years ago. Allan Coffman finances one thousand 7" vinyl copies of Mötley Crüe's first 45rpm single, Stick To Your Guns backed with Toast Of The Town, to be flung out for free at gigs and available to buy. The third song recorded Nobody Knows What It's Like To Be Lonely, formerly titled I Got The Power, isn't used. The cover bears a Nikki Sixx designed Mötley Crüe logo. The photos on the back cover are taken by Don Adkins Jr. in his parents' house. At Nikki's suggestion, Vince tries to hide his black eye by covering it with his hair.

When the band members have sex with girls in the studio, they visit the Southern California 24-hour fast-food Mexican restaurant chain Naugles on their way home to their ladies, and smear their Egg Burritos over their loins to disguise any scent of their infidelities.

24/4/81

Mötley Crüe performs their debut gigs, opening two sold-out shows on the same night for Oakland's Yesterday & Today (Y&T) at the Starwood on the corner of Crescent Heights and Santa Monica Boulevard in West Hollywood. Working at the club during the day, Nikki organised the support slot with the owner David Forest, who also managed his previous band London. The band works hard stapling posters on walls and lamp-posts around Hollywood to promote their shows and Nikki's rule is if a band has one poster, Mötley needs four. The band has never run through a full set in rehearsals before and doesn't know the set list until Nikki tapes a handwritten sheet of paper to the stage floor at the last minute. Forest books ten to twelve bands a week at the Starwood and this show is the first in years that he actually watches all of the band's set. The tale is told that a guy in the crowd spits on Vince during the first song Take Me To The Top, so he jumps off stage and puts him in a headlock, while Nikki smashes his bass into the shoulder of another punter keen on giving the Crüe trouble. Tommy joins in and hits him between the eyes with a drumstick, while Vince then hits him with a torch. In years to come, this tale is seen as a publicity tactic. The girlfriend of Randy Piper from W.A.S.P., Bella, is hired to film the shows from the club's balcony, but keeps the tape since she is not paid. These black and white videos of the Crüe's first live shows are still available in bootleg circles today.

25/4/81
Mötley plays two more shows this Saturday night opening for Y&T. By the end of their second performance, the Crüe has the crowd screaming for more and Y&T find themselves playing to a half-empty crowd. Mötley's stage attire includes a black telephone cord that Nikki wraps around his t-shirt.

15/5/81
The Crüe supports Stormer at the two-hundred-capacity Pookie's sandwiches and beer shop on Holly St in Pasadena. A roadie drives Tommy's van away before their stage clothes are unloaded, so they play their first set in their street clothes. An audience of twelve people is said to have watched the show while the Crüe consumes $137 worth of beer.

6/6/81
Mötley plays their first show at the Troubadour and set a new attendance record at the club. David Lee Roth from Van Halen takes a real liking to the band and introduces their set to the crowd. He chats with Vince after the show and they meet up the following afternoon at Canter's Deli on Fairfax, where Dave pulls up in his black Mercedes with a big skull and crossbones painted on its hood, and he proceeds to impart some of his knowledge of the music business upon Vince.

16/6/81

The band moves up to Allan Coffman's hometown of Grass Valley after he feels they should play some gigs there for practice. They call the shows the Anywhere USA tour and they sleep in Coffman's guest trailer and hitchhike into the town. It's said that the shows in 350-600 seat theatres are a sellout, due to their self-promotion.

19/6/81

Mötley plays at The Tommyknacker, not realising the night is themed as a Hollywood costume night. After getting zero response from the crowd playing Stick To Your Guns and Live Wire, they play Elvis Presley covers Jailhouse Rock and Hound Dog, the latter being played five times throughout the evening. After the gig they head to a party, where Vince scores a bag of cocaine from one of the drag queens present. He heads to the bathroom to shoot it up and realises it's baby powder. A huge brawl follows after the drag queen refuses to refund him his twenty dollars and Vince draws blood with a punch in his face.

20/6/81

The band attends their very first radio interview, sporting black eyes and fat lips from the brawl the previous night.

6/81

Determined to break the dependency of his girlfriend Leah, Vince escapes from her by piling his clothes into Tommy's van early one morning while she sleeps – he never sees her again. The band tells him that if he shoots up one more time he'll be out of the band, after arriving at a Country Club gig almost an hour late.

The band rehearses about nine songs every day at Visions Recording Studio in Burbank, which Mick's former Whitehorse band-mate Harry Clay has just bought. Their second-ever photo shoot takes place in the living room of Don Adkins Jr's parent's home. A blue tarpaulin purchased at the La Mirada Swapmeet is used as a backdrop, and Nikki has the idea to use balloons to create a party vibe. Mick's black Les Paul guitar is decorated with yellow safety perimeter tape, just prior to the shoot. Don lends Nikki one of his camera straps to wear as a sash across his chest.

Later in the month, Coffman finances a two-bedroom apartment at the rear of 1140 N. Clark Street, about four hundred feet from the Whisky a Go-Go for Tommy, Nikki and Vince to live in. The apartment #205 in the Sunset Terrace West complex is soon affectionately dubbed The Mötley House. They agree to rotate bedrooms every month but Nikki always has the bigger one to himself, while Tommy and Vince share the other. Their room has a mirror on the back of its door until one night it falls on David Lee Roth while he's preparing his drugs (and he doesn't spill any). Tommy puts a leather couch and a stereo that his parents gave him at Christmas in the front room. The only dishes they own are two drinking glasses and one plate in the cockroach-infested kitchen. Vince puts his electrical skills to good use by going onto the roof and splicing into another apartment's cable TV. Mick lives in Apartment D, 323 N. Gertruda Ave, Redondo Beach with his blonde, guitar-playing girlfriend Linda 'Windy' Correia and is still driven to and from rehearsals by his mate Stick. The Crüe's allowance is spent on rent, clothes and booze, while their food is dependent on the generous girls they pick up and Tommy's shoplifting skills. After a while, the rotting brown front door of the apartment doesn't shut properly after the police kick it in. The front window is smashed by a fire extinguisher thrown through it by Tommy's girlfriend Lisa.

20/7/81
Manager Allan Coffman continues to try and grow Mötley's standards of business professionalism and maintain common goals amongst all band members and management. He instructs the band members in writing to substantially curtail their drinking of alcohol and indicates they are each responsible for keeping themselves in top physical condition. A system of fines is imposed: ten dollars for showing up late to rehearsals and

twenty dollars for showing up hung-over, twenty dollars for any non-band member attending rehearsals, ten dollars for faulty equipment and instruments, twenty dollars for ignoring a management memo, and the loss of one week's advance for any physical or violent actions.

He also writes constructive suggestions to each member, telling Tommy that he is to develop and perform a drum solo beginning with their next gig, and his hair is to be done in a certain way before each performance. Vince is also told to take care of his personal appearance at all times, along with being instructed to take stock of his stage clothes since there is no longer a variety in his live attire. A ten-dollar fine is imposed for every time he misses a future vocal lesson. Coffman encourages Mick to communicate with him more, instead of remaining silent on issues he is unhappy with, while Nikki is instructed that all future communications need to be turned over to management to create management-to-management relationships, rather than artist-to-management ones.

8/81

Mötley's stage show continues to develop and grow, helped by them renting as much equipment from SIR as their budget allows, to make their stage shows look bigger. Coffman also rents Cadillacs for the band to travel around in; the Crüe damages the vehicles with their recklessness. Vince and Tommy briefly help Richard Crouch make a tiered drum riser with fifteen flashing lights in it wired by Vince, after being inspired by Queen. Years later, they sell it to their friends in Ratt who feature it in their Round and Round video clip. Allan Coffman hires Elvira for five hundred dollars to introduce Mötley Crüe on stage for one show. Nikki starts to light his leather stiletto boots on fire by splashing an isopropyl rubbing alcohol mix on them and igniting them, since his friend Blackie Lawless had stopped doing it as he was tired of burning himself. Mick buys a dozen lights from Don Dokken, while an old stained bed sheet of Tommy's is turned into a Mötley Crüe backdrop.

It's around this time that the band makes their first video clips, capturing live performances of Take Me To The Top and Public Enemy #1 at International Rehearsal Studios. Bell Piper Production performs the video and camera work on the clips, before they are edited by Tony Corrente at Music Lab.

Don Adkins photographs the band during an in-store appearance at Goodman Music.

Covers appearing in the set list include The Beatles' Paperback Writer and Elvis' Hound Dog mixed with Jailhouse Rock, and Savoy Brown's 1976 song My Babe. Another song played is Two Timer from Scorpions drummer Herman Rarebell's 1981 solo album Nip in the Bud. The Mötley song Merry-Go-Round emerges as a favourite amongst crowds. Nikki wrote the song about a guy in his early-twenties that he came across when he lived in Seattle. Nikki watched him sitting on a merry-go-round at some apartments before being taken away in a straight jacket after losing his mind from the pressures of life. The songs Why You Killing Yourself and Nobody Knows What It's Like To Be Lonely are phased out of the band's set, while On My Radio (formerly titled On My Video) and Straight To Hell never see the light of day.

9/9/81

A drunk Nikki and Vince arrive early for their show at the Whisky a Go-Go. Someone makes a distasteful remark to Nikki, so he smashes the guy's head into the bar, smashing glass and drawing blood. A bouncer walks the two band members upstairs where a girl at the bar jerks off Nikki. Upon leaving the club, Nikki finds Vince passed out under a car, so he drags him home only to find one of Tommy's female leftovers handcuffed to his bed. After passing out, Vince soon wakes up and the girl is gone from his bed, so they all head to a party at the Hyatt House. Nikki has sex in a closet with a drunk, huge-breasted girl, before inviting Tommy in on the action without her knowledge. Nikki then gets an unwilling young partygoer to join in the game as well, who loses his virginity in the process.

10/9/81

Not initially recalling the previous night's drunken events, Nikki is phoned by the girl from the closet last night, who tells him she was raped by a guy in his car after hitching a ride home after the party. Relieved that he didn't do it, but upon thinking of what he had done to the girl earlier, Nikki realises he perhaps went too far the night before.

3/10/81

Vince's looks continue to bring comparisons to David Lee Roth from Van Halen, who jams onstage to Jailhouse Rock at the Troubadour with Mötley. The band surprise Tommy on his nineteenth birthday with a cream pie fight on stage before the encore.

12/10/81

Mötley Crüe members sign music publishing agreements with Kim Fowley's Rare Magnetism Music for the publishing rights and royalty management of their songs.

31/10/81

Vince gets into a fight on Halloween at the Rainbow Bar and Grill. He gets arrested and locked up on a battery charge. It's around this time that voice teacher Gloria Bennett gives Vince six lessons for proper vocal technique at her Santa Monica Boulevard studio. He later has further coaching to learn proper vocal warm-ups and breathing techniques, enabling him to sing lots of shows in a week without losing his voice.

9/11/81

As preparation for the recording and release of the band's debut independent album, Mötley Crüe and Coffman & Coffman enter into a Limited Partnership Agreement. The six-page agreement details the formation of the partnership for the purpose of operating a record company Leathür Records, duration of the agreement, splits, and percentages. Allan Coffman uses an eight-page Limited Partner Agreement from

July 1969 as the template for this contract. Although both Mötley Crüe and Leathür Records have been in existence for nearly six months, neither the band name nor the record company name were formally registered until Coffman registers them in Nevada County, California. The name is thought up in a local Denny's coffee shop and changed from the spelling Leather Records, after this preference is already registered.

11/81
After breaking up with girlfriend Laurie Bell, and then a tall, blonde German fashion model Evelyn Roth, Nikki dates a blonde groupie named Beth for a couple of months, whom he met at the Troubadour one night as she used to be the girlfriend of Robbin Crosby from Ratt. From a rich family in San Diego, Nikki enjoys doing drugs and having sex at her apartment. After they party hard with Vince at the Rainbow one night, they then head back to The Mötley House on Clark Street, intent on having a threesome at Nikki's suggestion. Very keen on Beth, Vince blocks Nikki out, so he gets annoyed and heads to his room, and Beth Lynn becomes Vince's new girlfriend.

Mötley Crüe records their Too Fast For Love debut album over a drunken four days at Hit City West Studios on the corner of Pico and La Cienega boulevards. The time in the 24/16 track studio costs them sixty dollars per hour as a special after-hours room rate extended to Vince. They quickly fire the studio's engineer when he wants his own rate above and beyond this room rate. German producer Michael Wagener is brought to the helm of the brand-new Soundcraft 2400 series console board, having previously been in the metal band Accept and recently engineered and mixed their album Breaker; he has also previously worked with Judas Priest in the studio.

12/81
Too Fast For Love costs six thousand dollars to produce, which is advanced by Coffman and later paid back with proceeds from live shows. Since they are still an unsigned act, they release the album on their own Leathür Records label. The first pressing

sees two thousand copies produced with white lettering on the front cover and a close up picture of Vince's crotch, with one hand forming a sign some say means the devil's horns, while the deaf recognise it as hand language meaning 'I love you'.

A friend of Coffman's named Michael Pinter flies in from San Francisco to take the photos for the back cover. Vince is concerned with his hair not showing in the photos, since they are photographed with a white background. So it is touched up to make his innocent tease look like he's wearing a beehive toupee, which infuriates him as he only finds out once it's too late to change it. Mick also feels uneasy with the photos used, feeling he looks too much like Joan Jett of The Runaways.

The album is initially available at gigs and some record stores that the band members take them to. Allan Coffman also distributes a lot of copies himself, driving from store to store in his Lincoln rental car. Mike Flaherty, a fifth owner in Leathür Records and Crüe promoter as engaged by Coffman, also assists. Thanks are given inside the album to Skull and Cross Bones for their unselfish dedication – two Mötley roadies named Barry McQueary and Mark Ramirez respectively.

While celebrating the album's release with a party at The Troubadour, Runaways guitarist Lita Ford introduces herself to Nikki, who initially says his name is Rick. His attitude changes when she says she wants to shares her drugs with him, so she bites a Quaalude and puts a half in Nikki's mouth; their courtship begins.

Mötley Crüe is first played on the radio by disc jockey Michelle Nuval on KROQ one Sunday night.

The second pressing of Too Fast For Love has red lettering on the cover and a white label on the vinyl, not to mention a fixed-up Vince Neil hairdo. Four thousand copies are pressed and sold. Five thousand copies of the recording are also produced on cassette.

Nikki gets a tattoo of a black rose design, inked on his right upper arm by Kevin Brady at Sunset Strip Tattoo. The design also includes a small spider in a web.

Mick includes the use of blood capsules in his mouth during his stage performance for some shows.

25/12/81
The Crüe steals some turkey potpies from the liquor store cater-corner to the Whisky and hang beer cans, panties, snot and hypodermic needles on a stolen tree for Christmas. They set the tree alight with gasoline before leaving for their show at the Country Club. Vince has a Santa suit made for the show but declines to wear it on stage at the last minute as tensions between he and Nikki increase. This soon leads to Nikki wanting another singer. Stephen Pearcy rehearses with Mötley and is offered the position but he declines, preferring to stay in his band Ratt.

31/12/81
Mötley Crüe plays the Troubadour this New Year's Eve. David Lee Roth agrees to perform Jailhouse Rock with the band as an encore but disc jockey Michelle Nuval, with whom Crüe manager Allan Coffman is having an affair with, hops on stage and sings it with Vince instead, just as David Lee Roth makes his way to the stage. Nikki currently dates a redhead named Lynn Pierre, while Mike Flaherty dates her sister Tina.

1982

1/82

Vince Neil is arrested at the Troubadour after punching out a female patron, who takes offence at the official US Marines uniform he is wearing.

29/1/82

An international distribution deal is signed with Greenworld Records Ltd, which helps spread the Crüe's debut album throughout the United States and to the UK, where it receives rave reviews. This six-page contract grants Greenworld the right to license, manufacture, advertise, distribute and sell the Too Fast For Love album from their Torrance, California headquarters. Twenty thousand copies of a third pressing of Too Fast For Love are manufactured and distributed, this time with red lettering on the cover and a black label on the vinyl. Greenworld later goes bankrupt in 1986 but spawns Enigma Records.

The band and their manager are interviewed live at midnight on the top-rated Los Angeles rock radio station 95.5 KLOS with Joe Benson.

Record store employee Vicky Hamilton works out a management consulting role with Mötley's manager Allan Coffman, so she starts doing display merchandising for the album, putting up posters advertising the album in all the record stores around town.

11/2/82

As Nikki Sixx and Vince Neil leave the Rainbow with girlfriends Lita Ford and Beth Lynn, some bikers start pushing their girlfriends around after making advances on them. Displeased with the treatment handed out to his girlfriend, Nikki removes a chain from his waist and wields it around in the air during the fight that begins in the carpark between the

Rainbow and The Roxy. Two undercover police officers arrive, one of them grabbing Nikki's hand as he reaches for his chain, and biting it to the bone. Not realising it is a cop, Nikki retaliates by hitting him across the face with his chain until the cop pulls his gun on him to arrest him. They hit Nikki in the face with their clubs seven times, fracturing a cheekbone and giving him a black eye in the process. Vince runs off as Nikki is driven to the West Hollywood Police Station, but the cops stop in an alley on the way and repeatedly kick Vince in the stomach and face. Charged with assaulting a police officer with a deadly weapon, the police tell Nikki they will send him to state prison for five years, with no parole or probation. The incident is dubbed the sequel to Riot on Sunset Strip.

12/2/82

Nikki spends the night in jail before Lita hocks her Firebird TransAm for one thousand dollars and gives the money to the cops, who drop the charges. They walk the three miles back from the police lock-up to The Mötley House in time for their show at the Whisky. Nikki only has to wear black eye makeup on one eye for a while.

The concert is the first for Nikki's new seventeen-and-a-half-year-old bass tech Tim Luzzi, as they play the Whisky three nights in a row.

2/82

Mötley continues to sell out shows at the Troubadour, the Whisky and the Country Club. Crüe gloves are now available through mail-order in the U.S. as record stores continue to sell out of their debut album. One store even has a painting of Vince on the wall outside. Mötley invites lots of record companies to shows, but are shown no interest, even though they have sold thousands of albums within four months.

British rock magazine Kerrang! publishes the first magazine photo of a Mötley Crüe member: a full-page, full-colour picture of Vince. The Crüe is rumoured to tour the U.K. late in March and early April as the support act for Wishbone Ash but it never eventuates. Another rumour in the press says the Crüe will perform a co-headlining tour with Anvil in August, including playing the Reading Festival but it also does not eventuate.

12/3/82
The Los Angeles Department of Health Services issues an official notice of violation to Nikki Sixx for the non-removal of rubbish from The Mötley House.

3/82
At The Mötley House, Nikki writes lyrics for a song called Knock 'Em Dead Kid about his recent run-in with the Los Angeles Police outside the Rainbow. The following morning, an eviction notice is served by a lawyer, bringing The Mötley House days to an end after nine months of complete mayhem. Nikki moves into Lita Ford's residence at Apartment 6, 4859 Coldwater Canyon, Sherman Oaks in North Hollywood, while Vince moves into Beth's apartment one block east. Mick is still living with his girlfriend Linda in Redondo Beach.

Tommy Lee moves into a small house with a pool in the backyard with his new Canadian stripper girlfriend and Penthouse Pet named Candice Starrek, having recently dumped Lisa for her. They met when Tommy was helping a stripper friend of Nikki's to move into Candice's house. Candice was seeing Greg Guiffria from the band Angel at the time, who also lived at the house. Tommy asked Candice to come and see him play with Mötley at the Whisky A Go-Go about three weeks ago and they have been seeing each other since.

Tommy and Vince give new band Metallica a major break, as they help them land a support performance with Saxon at the Whisky for their second gig. They introduce Metallica's bass player Ron McGovney to the Whisky's booking agent, who locks in their performance after hearing a demo tape.

8/4/82
Mötley plays a sold-out show at the three-and-a-half-thousand-seat capacity Santa Monica Civic, which is produced by racing

car promoter Steve Quercio, who has seen them play the Whisky and wanted to help get them to the next level. The evening is compered by Elvira and Mötley shares the stage with a couple of Funny Cars owned by John Force. As they play, they set fire to various instruments, set off thirty two red smoke bombs, and debut their new song Knock 'Em Dead Kid. The performance and number of ticket sales for a local Hollywood club band finally attracts the attention of record labels and the event becomes a turning point for the Crüe.

4/82
Tom Zutaut, a sales assistant at Elektra Records, heads out for a bite to eat at a coffee shop on Sunset Boulevard one night, when he sees a huge crowd of kids trying to get into the Whisky a Go-Go, underneath a marquee that says "Mötley Crüe Sold Out." He then notices a Mötley display in the shop window of record store Licorice Pizza on the corner, which was created by Vicky Hamilton and featured mannequin parts holding their album cover, along with tarot cards, whips, chains, handcuffs, and a pair of dirty female underpants from Vince that were left by a girl he was with the night before. Telling the club's owner Mario Maglieri at the door that he is an A&R representative for Elektra, Zutaut makes his way inside the Whisky and is impressed by the show in front of five hundred punters. He talks with Allan Coffman afterwards about having the band come into Elektra for a meeting, who refers him onto their distributor, Greenworld. Visiting their booth at a local trade show, Greenworld's Alan Niven puts Zutaut back in touch with Allan Coffman. After first rejecting Zutaut's request to sign the band, Elektra chairman, Joe Smith agrees to allow him to sign the band, so he wines and dines the band on his company expense account until they are about to sign.

7/5/82
Virgin Records staff sees a great show at Glendale Civic Centre billed as "An evening of thrills and chills with the original boys of metal madness: Mötley Crüe" and offers to sign them. The

band receives a performance fee of four thousand dollars for the night's show. Virgin then brings a briefcase filled with ten thousand dollars as a cash advance on a one hundred thousand dollar deal to a meeting with the band, and tells them all about how their label operates out of England.

Wearing a Crüe construction hat, Vince now starts to cuts the head off mannequins on stage with a chainsaw during Piece Of Your Action, which is the first track Mick plays slide guitar on.

13/5/82

W.A.S.P. headlines a Friday the 13th concert at Perkins Palace in Pasadena with Ratt and Armored Saint in support, which is promoted by Gina Zamparelli. Nikki is a special guest and joins W.A.S.P. on stage to play I Wanna Be Somebody.

5/82

Mick gets his first tattoo: a small scorpion design on his right hand inked by Robert Benedetti at Sunset Strip Tattoo. It is later detailed further by Sunset Strip's Greg James. As Mick now starts to become well known in the Crüe, Michelle Meyers, the last vocalist in his former band Whitehorse who used the stage name Micki Marz, tries to sue him for stealing her 'thunder', as she is receiving favourable reviews for her performances around Los Angeles in a Janis Joplin tribute band. The meteoric rise of the Crüe overwhelms her complaint and she bitterly leaves the music industry.

Tom Zutaut puts a comparable offer on the table to that of Virgin Records. The band says they will accept the deal from the local Los Angeles base of Elektra, over the Virgin offer of about twenty five thousand dollars more. A celebration at Mexican Restaurant Casa Cugats follows, where band manager Allan Coffman gets drunk and starts thinking he's back in Vietnam. After ripping a payphone off the wall, Tom Zutaut drives him back to his hotel room, but not before he rolls out of the car in the middle of the intersection of La Cienega and Santa Monica Boulevard, crawling on his belly like a soldier

with a rifle. Zutaut calls Mick the Purple People Eater as he says
he has a purple aura.

20/5/82

Mötley Crüe signs their record deal with Elektra Records; a 41-
page agreement between Elektra Records and the four band
members that details the terms and condition related to their
new seven-year engagement. A further four-page Royalty and
Advance Agreement between Elektra and the band members is
also signed as an agreement to the splits, royalties and advances
for the re-release of Too Fast For Love, as well as the next five
albums to which the band contractually obligates itself. An
advance cheque for $28,500 is received as part of the execution
payment for the agreement. This follows the signing of an
eleven-page agreement between Greenworld and Elektra
Records to transfer the Too Fast For Love license from
Greenworld to Elektra Records.

They celebrate with a dinner at Benihana on La Cienega
Boulevard. After drinking the heaviest throughout the night,
Vince keeps biting and cracking his margarita glass as he hassles
the waitress. The manager kicks them out while the waitress
calls the police.

Annoyed that Zutaut had gone over his head to sign the
band, Elektra's head of A&R, Kenny Buttice, convinces the
label that the Too Fast For Love album needs to be remixed
before they release it, so it is up to radio standards. Roy Thomas
Baker is chosen to perform the work; he has previously
produced classic albums with Journey, Foreigner, the Cars and
Queen. Vince re-records his vocals and the whole album is remixed at RTB's house in the hills on Sunset Drive. Roy throws
huge parties full of sex, drugs and rock'n'roll, which Mötley
takes a liking to.

With his limited experience in the music industry, Crüe
manager Allan Coffman feels he needs further assistance to take
the band to the next level. Elektra Records also places pressure
on him, as they now want to hand the band over to a major
management company. He decides he needs someone with

experience in radio and touring, and subsequently hooks up with Bill Larson, a young Michigan concert promoter with a background in radio promotions. Coffman's house is mortgaged to cover the band's expenses, and he sees an opportunity to sell some of his fifteen percent ownership in Mötley Crüe Inc.

3/6/82

As the remixing of Too Fast For Love nears completion, Allan Coffman and his assistant of four months, Eric Greif (who also manages Greg Leon), decide a Crüesing Through Canada tour will provide Mötley with valuable road experience, and possibly keep them out of trouble on the Los Angeles streets for a while. The tour is designed to have maximum controversial impact to gain important media attention from outside L.A. Coffman plans to meet up with Bill Larson after the tour and bring the band to Detroit for a welcome back to the U.S.A. show. The Crüe flies north, as their luggage travels by truck with the roadies. Vince forgets to include his luggage on the truck, so he has to take it on the plane. Nikki instructs the band members to wear their stage gear on the plane and when they land at Edmonton International Airport, Canada's federal police and Immigration officials interrogate them for over three hours. They confiscate around two thousand dollars worth of stage gear, including whips, chains, studded belts and spiked wristbands, deeming them to be 'dangerous weapons.' Vince's small bag of Playboy and Hustler magazines is also confiscated. The road entourage is delayed for around seven hours as Canadian border guards search for contraband. The small Calgary booking agency, Performing Artists Consultants, had told them to be expecting to play 800-1700 seat halls depending on whom they were supporting, but on arrival they find no such venues booked. Coffman knew the venues were small but never let on to the band.

7/6/82

Booked at Scandals Disco in the Edmonton Sheraton Caravan Hotel, the Crüe plays four sets. Rudy Sarzo and Don Airey from Ozzy Osbourne's band watch the show. Nikki has a beer bottle thrown at him, which cuts open his right hand. He keeps playing while throwing blood onto the small crowd. A guy goes to take a swing at Tommy backstage between sets, but ends up having his teeth knocked out by Allan Coffman's knee. Coffman breaks a finger in the fight. Nikki tells an interviewer backstage, "We're going to be huge because we're entertainment. Our next album will be called Television and Violence. We're the television. Our audience is the violence. Together, we'll take over the world!"

8/6/82

Mötley Crüe is rushed by police to evacuate their show after a call is made threatening to "waste the band on stage." Six policemen arrive and search the complex, and once satisfied, allow them to continue to play. The Crüe members refuse to play unless the police are present, so two policemen stand vigil by each side of the stage as they finish their set. Decades later, it is revealed that the death threat call was actually made by Allan Coffman's assistant Eric Greif to the Edmonton Sun newspaper as a successful publicity stunt for nationwide press and great stories to tell back in the States.

10/6/82

The manager of the Sheraton and two bodyguards waiting at the Riviera Rock Room where the Crüe is about to play, demand two hundred and sixty dollars for damage caused to a trashed eighth floor of their hotel. The bill is cheap considering a bored Tommy threw a small Sony television out the window of his room onto the pavement below.

After playing their last two nights in Edmonton, Coffman ends the tour because he had run out of money to keep it going. The remaining shows in British Columbia are cancelled and the Crüe returns home to L.A. amid national press coverage on the horrific exploits of the American band. The booking agent considers suing the Crüe for a million dollars. Eric Greif wears the financial brunt of the cancellation since he took personal responsibility for the gigs through his company Kondor Recording and Production. By the time the band's confiscated stage clothes are approved for return, the items have already been destroyed.

1/7/82
Elektra Records proposes a two-page addendum to the band's record contract detailing their intention to decrease royalties just six weeks after the contract's signing, but the band doesn't sign it.

2/7/82
A Scandinavian tour for the first two weeks of August is negotiated with a Finland agency but the tour doesn't eventuate.

7/82
Vince is the last Mötley member to get a tattoo. His first inking is of a snake with a musical note on his upper left arm.

Tom Zutaut calls Doug Thaler at Contemporary Communications Corp. in Manhattan to try and get Mötley on the bill for the forthcoming Aerosmith tour, but Doug has just added an old agency client of his to the tour in Pat Travers.

Mötley promotes their next shows back in Los Angeles at the Country Club with a new photo of the band taken by Debra Meyers, featuring a large white on black pentagram backdrop, candelabras, skulls on sticks, dry ice, and Nikki holding a red smoke bomb.

16/8/82
Live Wire is the first release on Elektra for the band. The 7" single is backed with Take Me To The Top and Merry-Go-Round, as the Crüe is back playing to big crowds in Los Angeles again.

Nikki meets Alice Cooper for the first time, who is working on his new album Zipper Catches Skin in a neighbouring studio at Cherokee in Hollywood. Alice is holding scissors when they meet, which are later heard as an effect in the song Tag, You're It from the album.

20/8/82

The Too Fast For Love album is re-released on Elektra and enters the Billboard chart at #157. A few changes to the album cover are made with the front photo and logo being enlarged and the rear album photo getting reduced. A new band picture by Debra Meyers is included on the lyric sheet inside. The song Stick To Your Guns is omitted from this new version. Nikki instructs Tom Zutaut to ensure the song Toast of the Town is excluded, so Kim Fowley will not make any money from publishing of the release. Kim told Tom that Nikki begged him for $500, so he gave him the money in return for the publishing of Toast of the Town, but Nikki felt Kim took advantage of him during a weak drug-impaired moment as a starving kid on the streets. In Canada only, Elektra releases the original Leathür version of the songs with a re-vamped Too Fast For Love cover. Around five hundred Canadian promo copies of the album are pressed, along with 1-2 thousand regular copies.

Elektra's promotional priority is Australian band Cold Chisel, and after a lack of support for Mötley is shown, the label's head of promotions is fired. Tom Werman is brought in to Elektra as head of A&R around this same time and he instantly clicks with Nikki.

26/8/82

After performing shows at The Roxy the last two nights, which were promoted with a tagline of "Hell's Revenge - from the boys you love to hate", Mötley starts to demo songs for their next album, including Looks That Kill, Hotter Than Hell, Knock 'Em Dead Kid, Red Hot and Running Wild.

9/9/82

Mötley performs at The Keystone in Palo Alto, California with Saxon and Trauma, the latter band featuring a bass player named Cliff Burton who goes on to join Metallica.

29/9/82

Under the Power of Attorney in his management contract, Allan Coffman sells five percent of his fifteen percent stake in Mötley Crüe to Bill Larson for twenty five thousand dollars, which he acquires from the life savings of his parents; his father being a retired school professor and his Swedish mother, a housewife. Twenty-one-year-old Larson drives from Davison, Michigan and stays with Coffman for a couple of days, before they head into Los Angeles where they meet with industry executives. Larson meets the band at SIR Rehearsal Studios, but Coffman does not tell them what the arrangement is.

10/82

Mötley does a photo shoot with Mark Weiss and interview for porn magazine Oui. Afterwards, Tommy disappears for three days with one of the female models. The article and pictures are published in the November 1982 issue of the magazine with Cheryl Rixon on the cover.

31/10/82

The Crüe plays an awesome Halloween show at the Concord Pavilion in San Francisco with Y&T and Jimi Hendrix impersonator Randy Hansen and the Machine Guns in support. Three new songs are performed for the first time: Looks That Kill, Shout At The Devil (written at Lita Ford's mother's dining table in Long Beach as she cooked dinner) and Red Hot. During the encore song Red Hot, Nikki walks over to a candelabra on stage and touches his shoulder to the candle's flame, instantly igniting his leather jumpsuit while he continues to play. Within seconds, the Concord Fire Department gets on stage putting Nikki out and subsequently fines the band one thousand dollars for starting the fire on stage, since it was against their orders.

1/11/82

Wishing to clarify his position with Mötley Crüe, Bill Larson makes copies of his legal agreements he had entered into with Allan Coffman, and gives them to Mötley's merchandise guy. He in turn gives them to Nikki and Mick who don't realise that Larson's percentage was provided out of Coffman's share, and they think that Coffman is ripping them off. Miscommunication and misunderstanding aside, the trust is broken and Coffman makes an attempt to provide a workable solution where he removes himself from the band as a shareholder but remains involved as a personal manager for the next three years. In exchange for this transaction, Coffman seeks financial compensation for his investments of the past eighteen months, all to no avail as the Personal Management Agreement dated this day is never reached.

12/82

A video clip is made for Mötley's single Live Wire. An unreleased video of Take Me To The Top is also filmed and edited very similarly to Live Wire, also displaying the Crüe's live stage show at the time.

Mötley begins recording their second album at The Annex in Northridge with Jeffers Dodge engineering, which Nikki wants to call Shout With The Devil, as he and Lita fool around with satanic black magic. They record songs that include the unreleased Run For Your Life, Running Wild In The Night and I Will Survive. One night Nikki, Tommy and his drum tech, Clyde 'the Spide' Duncan, get hassled by a couple of policemen as they have a few drinks in a bar around the corner from a North Hollywood recording studio, so as they leave, they urinate through the open window into their patrol car before running off. Tommy throws a brick through the control room window upon returning to the studio, causing Jeffers to be banned from the facility even though it is managed by his

girlfriend. The following morning they work on the track I Will
Survive at The Annex. It is Nikki and Vince's idea to do some
backward masking, so they lay on their backs chanting into
microphones above, while Jeffers suspends a gong on a rope
above them, making a shimmering sound effect as it spins in
circles. When the half-track is played backwards they hear
"Jesus is Satan." Jeffers' second engineer disappears, found
hours later praying in the back forty of the ranch studio,
believing they are all possessed by Satan. The motor in
Tommy's car blows up as he drives home from this recording
session, while Mick pulls over because his car alarm comes on
and his lights keep flicking on and off. One of Nikki's picks
flies off the table in the studio and sticks in the ceiling. Tom
Zutaut witnesses a knife and fork rise off Nikki and Lita's table
and stick into the ceiling.

18/12/82
A week prior to Christmas, Allan Coffman is advised by an
attorney on the telephone to cease and desist as their manager.
Coffman has been trying to get them to stop taking drugs while
record company executives encourage it. He is also against
them progressing towards a more satanic image. The Crüe feels
he is not able to manage their success growth and they can't
understand where all the money from sell-out shows and the
record company advance is going. It also seems that he is
contributing substantial amounts of band money to the political
campaign of George Deukmajian, the arch conservative
Republican who runs for Governor. The news devastates
Coffman, who has mortgaged his home three times to pay for
the Crüe's stage show theatrics and other expenses, personally
contributing around three hundred thousand dollars over the
time of his management. Coffman files for Bankruptcy. Bill
Larson's association with the band also ends, as his contract is
tied in with Coffman's.

21/12/82

Allan Coffman takes his termination very hard. His wife
Barbara comes home to find her husband pacing their back
yard with a gun in his hand, contemplating suicide. He later gets
divorced from her and marries another lady named Barbara and
becomes a born-again Christian. Bill Larson's father passes
away six months later, after suffering a heart attack from
worrying about the fate of his son and their lost life savings. Bill
suffers clinical depression for a couple of years following the
incident and eventually files a lawsuit to try and get his twenty
five thousand dollars back, but it is thrown out of court as no-
one is able to find Coffman to serve the subpoena. Bill Larson
continues to work in the music industry and goes on to become
a co-founder of HardRadio. Mick's friend and band production
guy John 'Stick' Crouch is also ousted from the Crüe camp, due
to his relationship with Coffman.

31/12/82

L.A's own black leather demons Mötley Crüe plays a show in
front of three thousand people called New Year's Evil at the
Santa Monica Civic Auditorium, said to be one of the greatest
glam shows ever! Currently without a manager, Mötley is
assisted by Barry Levine as a creative consultant/manager, and
in-turn introduces photographer friend Neil Zlozower to the
band who begins shoots them. Levine also helps them to invite
as many potential managers as possible to see the show, as they
feel this performance is a do-or-die event in their careers. Big
Crüe fan, Ronnie James Dio, tips off his booking agent friend
Doug Thaler about the Crüe. Doug played in Ronnie Dio and
The Prophets back in the late-sixties before almost losing his
leg when their tour van was involved in a head-on collision in
Massachusetts. Pat Travers' manager Doc McGhee is keen for
Doug to join his company, so they both attend the Mötley
showcase from Florida and love it. They ride home in an empty
merchandise truck after the entire product is sold. Santa Monica
authorities ban the proposed Miss Nude Heavy Metal prelude,
citing laws prohibiting "depravity of minors", as a band called

The Wigglers open the show, featuring Vince's former Rockandi guitarist James Alverson. Before playing Red Hot, Vince says their next album will be called Theatre of Pain and out in March. The Crüe is fined one thousand dollars by the local fire marshals as they come off stage for the use of fire in their show, which included twenty-foot high mortars. Backstage, Nikki takes a black makeup pencil and walks over to a wasted Joe Perry from Aerosmith before smearing the pencil under his eyes, inspired by the Road Warrior characters in the film Mad Max. Joe thinks it looks cool on Nikki. Meanwhile Vince is in tears as his phone has been cut off, due to the band's desperate financial state.

1983

3/1/83

Vince Neil marries his fiancée Beth Lynn at the Crystal Cathedral church building in Garden Grove, Orange County, just near Disneyland. All members of the Crüe jam on Looks That Kill at the wedding reception.

26/1/83

Mötley Crüe's Too Fast For Love album is released in Australia, as the Live Wire video airs for the first time on U.S. TV. The first time Nikki sees the Live Wire video on TV is on the new cable show HBO.

2/83

The Crüe flies to Las Vegas on Doc McGhee's private plane to see how he runs his organisation, McGhee Entertainment Inc. The meeting arises after Doug Thaler and McGhee witnessed Mötley's mind-blowing show on New Year's Eve and are keen to manage them. Impressed and eager to play bigger shows, they soon agree that Doc and Doug will be Mötley's new management team and are pleased they come through when their chips are down. Doc's under-the-table gifts and masterly methods of manipulation soon ensure Mötley becomes more of a priority with Elektra Records.

3/83

Mötley's new management line up a string of dates as support act for Kiss. Doug Thaler attends the band's first pre-tour rehearsal, and feels each guy is twenty pounds overweight and instructs them to get in better shape before the shows commence in a few weeks. Returning from business in New York ten days later, Thaler sees each member down ten to fifteen pounds after rehearsing two sets every night. Barry Levine assists Mötley with their image via a number of photo shoots. He also works with them on video concepts and choreography, as well as marketing and merchandising consulting. Nikki buys himself a new Porsche 911SC after landing a publishing deal with Warner-Chappell.

26/3/83
Mötley opens their first support show for Kiss on the west coast leg of their Creatures of the Night tour at the 5,700-capacity Irvine Meadows Amphitheatre in California, playing a forty-minute set. The band members are excited at travelling on a tour bus for the first time, even though it breaks down for many hours on the way to their Phoenix show.

3/4/83
The Moral Majority tries to stop the Crüe and Kiss Easter performance at the San Francisco Civic Auditorium by pushing bike racks in front of the stage doors, to keep them from entering the venue. After five Kiss support shows celebrating their tenth anniversary, Gene Simmons kicks Mötley off the tour for bad behaviour, although Doug Thaler believes the decision is made because Mötley is upstaging Kiss' performance. The real reason is later revealed: Tommy and Nikki were caught having sex with Eric Carr's girlfriend behind the fox's drum kit in Phoenix, Arizona as he played Rock 'n' Roll All Nite.

4/83
Bob Krasnow takes over the reigns at Elektra following Joe Smith's termination and he replaces Tom Werman with Roy Thomas Baker. Werman is still keen to produce the new Mötley album, but just as they are about to go into the studio, Krasnow decides he wants to drop Mötley, as he feels rock'n'roll isn't happening anymore. He also instructs MTV to take Mötley's Live Wire video off the air, thinking it's an embarrassment to the record company with a tradition of such talented acts like Linda Ronstadt, The Doors and Jackson Browne. After

negotiations, Krasnow tells Mötley's management that he will put the album out, but make it easy for them to move on.

11/4/83

Known to the band for her work with Van Halen, clothing designer Fleur Thiemeyer is engaged by Mötley Crüe to come up with new stage clothes. After liking her initial sketches that look like a cross between Genghis Khan, medieval knights and barbaric warriors, they get together at her apartment on Ocean Ave, Santa Monica where they further refine sketches to redraw and colour the designs so they are exactly as they want.

5/83

Mötley works on recording their new album at Cherokee Studios with Geoff Workman engineering. The Doors' keyboardist, Ray Manzarek, records his Carmina Burana album in the next room and regularly parties with the Crüe and their cocaine. The sessions also have girls streaming in and out of the studio constantly. The introduction of the unreleased song Black Widow is re-worked into an instrumental titled God Bless The Children Of The Beast. A song Wild Dogs was brought in by Mick and worked on, but the lyrics were never recorded on the unreleased instrumental track. Nikki has a grand vision of the album and tour looking like a cross between a Nazi rally and a Black Mass service.

29/5/83

On Memorial Day long weekend, Mötley plays the huge three-day Us Festival on the outskirts of Los Angeles in Glen Helen Regional Park near Devore, San Bernardino, California. Mötley arrives at the festival by way of their first helicopter ride. Day two is Heavy Metal Day and Mötley plays second on stage at 12:30pm after Quiet Riot, in front of three hundred and seventy thousand people in the scorching spring heat. Tommy Lee passes out just before going on stage and requires oxygen to assist him. The band sees the concert as a great chance to test some of the new material they have just begun recording.

They're unhappy with their sloppy musical performance, but very pleased with the huge response from the crowd. After leaving the stage, they head back to their dressing room trailer and Mick's girlfriend Linda punches him in the face for no apparent reason, without saying a word. Vince then makes out with Tom Zutaut's date Ashley, much to Nikki's disapproval. Ozzy Osbourne, Judas Priest, Triumph, Scorpions and Van Halen follow Mötley's set on stage. The festival attracts one hundred and thirty arrests, and one murder over a drug deal. Acts including The Clash, Men at Work, David Bowie and The Pretenders play on the other two days. In time, Mötley's performance at this festival goes down as one of the most important and influential of their career.

The festival is the first show that Mötley has their own bodyguard: Fred Saunders is hired by management and becomes their Security Director. He previously worked in production for Avalon Attractions, the promoter of the band's large shows at Santa Monica Civic Auditorium and Perkins Palace.

6/83

Nikki goes to a party at Roy Thomas Baker's house in Hollywood with Tommy and his girlfriend Candice Starrek. They take heaps of drugs in the Jacuzzi at the party, including lines of cocaine off his glass top grand piano. Nikki joins Tommy and Candice in the Jacuzzi, along with a dozen or so naked others. When RTB locks-down the house so people can't leave in their intoxicated state, Nikki decides he wants to go and see Lita, but he can't find his clothes. He finds a way to scale the wall of RTB's house and drives off naked in his Porsche 911, as he had left the keys in the ignition. Two girls who couldn't get into the party chase him down the street in their '68 Mustang. As his speedometer clocks 90mph, he looks back to see if he has lost the girls, before slamming his Porsche into a telephone pole, which now sits next to him in the passenger's seat. Hitching a ride, the naked Nikki Sixx is picked up by a couple and driven to hospital, where his dislocated shoulder sustained in the accident is put back into place and into a sling, before he is sent home with a bottle of Percodan painkillers. Lita talks him into backing off from flirting with Satanism.

7/83

Nikki begins to smoke heroin with Vince to help numb the pain of his shoulder. They then have access to higher-grade smack by way of Gregory Boaz aka Smog Vomit, the bassist from local punk band Tex and the Horseheads, and their mutual friend, Robbin Crosby from Ratt. They show Nikki how to use needles, and he is soon inventing his own speedball combinations, realising that drugs are to be his vice for life. Vince prefers to chase the dragon instead, having stopped using needles when he left his former girlfriend Leah.

8/83

Blackie Lawless approaches the Crüe with a song he has written called Wild Child. Nikki feels the vocals are out of Vince's range for Mötley to use it, so Blackie retains it as a song for his band W.A.S.P. It is later released in 1985 as the opening track on their sophomore album The Last Command.

As work on the new Mötley album draws to a close, Nikki's shoulder is now fully healed. Seeing that other bands have now copied their glam-punk Too Fast For Love image, Mötley evolves their look with designer Fleur Thiemeyer into a cross between Mad Max and Escape From New York, two movies they watched many times while they lived together in The Mötley House. Nikki has a single studded shoulder pad made to look like a gas pirate from Mad Max, while he has thigh-high leather boots made with a cage in the heel to eject smoke at the press of a button. All of the larger-than-life boots for the band are custom-made by Di Fabrizio Shoes on Fairfax Ave, while buckles and chains are sourced from adult store The Pleasure Chest.

17/9/83

Mötley plays a huge show with Def Leppard, Uriah Heep and Eddie Money in front of fifty thousand people at San Diego's Qualcomm Stadium.

Around this time, a video is shot for the band's anticipated first single Looks That Kill, from the soon-to-be-released album. Nikki wrote the song with girlfriend Lita Ford in mind. Marcelo Epstein produces the video on a budget of seventy five thousand dollars, shot over two very long days on the lot of A&M Records on the main sound stage. Mick gets drunk on the set by drinking vodka out of his Coke can. The video's central female character is Wendy Barry from Los Angeles, who was the last girl to audition and gets paid about a hundred dollars for her first music video performance. The video is designed to shock and make viewers feel uncomfortable.

26/9/83

Mötley Crüe's Shout At The Devil album is released, selling two hundred thousand copies in its first two weeks and eventually reaching number seventeen on the charts. With its cover designed by Bob Defrin, the album contains the track Knock 'Em Dead Kid, dedicated to the L.A. Police Dept., and another song called Bastard, written about former manager Allan Coffman. There's also a cover version of The Beatles' classic Helter Skelter included. Mötley insists the album is not satanic, but about shouting AT the devil, not WITH. The instrumental God Bless The Children Of The Beast is inspired by the introduction on David Bowie's Diamond Dogs album. Sound Engineer Geoff Workman narrates the introductory track In The Beginning, even though the album's packaging says its band mascot Allister Fiend who narrates Nikki's lyrics. The song contains the lyric, "It has been written, 'Those who have the youth, have the future'" that is an adaption of "whoever has the youth has the future" written by Nazi leader Adolf Hitler in his book *Mein Kampf*. The album eventually goes on to sell over three million copies.

Acclaimed session keyboardist Jai Winding (who has worked on albums by Jackson Browne, Cheap Tick, Boz Scaggs, Dusty Springfield, Donna Summer, George Benson, and Molly Hatchet) is credited on the album, along with session synth player Paul Fox, formerly of the Ruts. Tom Kelly and Richard Page, who have both worked on albums by REO Speedwagon, Barry Manilow, Cher, Rick Springfield, America and Survivor, receive backing vocal credits for their work.

10/83
Tommy is currently living in a condo at 1734 North Fuller Street, Los Angeles with his girlfriend Candice.

29/10/83
At 2pm, the Crüe attends a personal in-store appearance at Tower Records in West Covina, California.

11/11/83
Mötley commences a twenty-three-city Shout At The Devil headlining tour with a sell-out show at the six-hundred-seat-capacity Orange Pavilion in San Bernadino. Axe from Florida and Heaven from Australia play as the support bands on the tour. The stage set represents a desolate debacle of civilisation, with a painted backdrop of a city skyline, based on the movie Escape from New York. Tommy's drum riser is constructed to look like rubble from an exploded freeway, while their amps are adorned with Styrofoam spikes. The set was built piece-by-piece in the backyard of Barry Levine's friend over a three-month period earlier in the year before he was fired. At the start of Mötley's set, one of the roadies enters the smoke-filled stage with a horror mask and mimes to a tape of someone reciting Edgar Allan Poe's poem from 1843 called The Conqueror Worm, where it says, "That Mötley drama – oh, be sure... it shall not be forgot."

The video for Looks That Kill is aired for the first time and the band flies between shows in Doc McGhee's eight-seat plane, with the plane nose-diving to the ground after an electrical malfunction one flight. The only real damage sustained is the Crüe's stage makeup and cleansers that explode in their luggage due to the sudden drop in cabin pressure.

16/12/83

The final show of the Shout At The Devil headlining tour takes place in Arizona. Vince and Tommy then head to the Cayman Islands for a two-week holiday.

31/12/83

In the Cayman Islands on New Year's Eve, Vince and Tommy jam with a local reggae band on I Shot The Sheriff at the island's Club Inferno. They then fly out to meet Nikki and Mick at Long View Farm rehearsal studio in North Brookfield, Massachusetts to start preparing for a tour support slot on Ozzy Osbourne's Bark At The Moon tour. At the farm, the band's limo drivers bring them copious amounts of drugs and hookers from Manhattan that they indulge in over the week-long stay. Under the influence, Nikki smashes his guitar on a few exit signs so he has to buy another one. The Rolling Stones had used the farm to rehearse in during 1981, and Aerosmith recorded Chip Away The Stone there in 1978.

1984

10/1/84

Mötley plays their opening show on the first leg of Ozzy Osbourne's Bark At The Moon tour in front of nine and a half thousand people in Portland, Maine. They meet Ozzy for the first time during his sound-check, and he instantly takes a liking to them. He hardly spends a night on his own tour bus, preferring to travel on the partying bus of the Crüe instead. Ozzy's photographer Ross Halfin takes many tour bus photos of them with groupies.

28/1/84

Tommy Lee sees snow for the first time in his life on tour in Buffalo, New York. Backstage after the show, he finds out that his girlfriend has posed for the current February issue of Penthouse magazine on newsstands without his knowledge, after a fan passes comment on the pictures. Tommy punches the fan unconscious with one hit, before Mötley's manager Doug Thaler convinces the fan not to press any charges.

29/1/84

At the Limelight Club in Manhattan, New York, the members of Mötley Crüe are awarded Gold albums for Shout At The Devil, signifying half a million copies sold.

30/1/84

After their Gold album presentation the previous night, Mötley is awarded Platinum albums on stage during their first-ever show at the famous Madison Square Garden in New York City. This is the band's first Platinum award, as they have now sold over a million copies of Shout At The Devil.

When Tommy walks into his condo with his Gold and Platinum awards for the first time after the tour, his girlfriend Candice throws a plate at him, smashing the glass framing of his

Gold award, enraged over a photo she found of Tommy engaged in a sexual act with some girls.

Nikki Sixx takes his awards with him to the island of Nantucket where he plans on meeting some girls, one of them actress Demi Moore who is working on the movie set of One Crazy Summer. Demi shared a similar childhood to that of Nikki in many ways, with her father leaving before she was born, then being around drinking, arguing and beatings, and moving home a ridiculous amount of times. She greets Nikki as the prop-plane lands, who in a wasted state, falls down the plane's steps onto the tarmac, smashing a bottle of Jack Daniels from his hand while his awards hit him in the head. Having been through Alcoholics Anonymous herself, Demi suggests the program to Nikki, who learns of it for the first time.

2/84

Mötley Crüe and Ozzy get up to all sorts of debauchery on tour. In Memphis, Ozzy, Tommy and Vince Neil nearly get arrested for urinating on a police car, after getting very drunk on sake and lying in the middle of a freeway. When they get back to the hotel, Ozzy defecates in Tommy's bathroom and wipes the faeces all over the walls in his room. When a concert is cancelled after Ozzy injures himself on the set shooting the video for his song So Tired, they still come through the town and do a radio interview. Ozzy and Vince notice keys in a car's ignition so they steal it and frighten pedestrians, before smashing its windows and ruining its upholstery. The Crüe is also attracting a lot of religious protesters due to their supposed worshipping of the devil.

4/2/84

Elektra releases Looks That Kill as the first single from Shout At The Devil, with Piece Of Your Action on the flipside. It spends ten weeks in the charts and peaks at number fifty four.

19/2/84

Mötley and Ozzy arrive in New Orleans on the second night of Mardi Gras. Vince and Ozzy check out some local strip clubs, while Tommy, Nikki and Jake E. Lee from Ozzy's band get themselves into a knife fight at a bar called Dungeon on Bourbon Street, After messing around with the girlfriend of the bar's bouncer, Nikki says they got thrown out and cut, as guys with spiked clubs were trying to smash them in the head.

22/2/84

Mötley arrives at their hotel for their show in Lakeland, Florida and head to the bar. Ozzy enters with a dollar bill placed between the cheeks of his ass, and offers it to other drinkers. He runs off with the bag of an elderly woman after she hassles him over his antics, and soon goes to the pool wearing a summer dress he finds in her bag. He soon tells Nikki that he feels like doing a line of cocaine, but they have none. So Ozzy then walks over and snorts a long line of ants up his nose before urinating on the pavement from under his dress, and licking it up. He challenges Nikki to copy him, who also urinates on the pavement, but before he has a chance to lick it up, Ozzy beats him to it.

24/3/84

While playing the final show of the first leg in support for Ozzy in Portland, Oregon, sixteen pounds of glittery flour is dropped from the lighting rig onto the heads of Mötley Crüe throughout their forty-five-minute set. As they leave the stage, Ozzy and his band-mates continue the attack by throwing custard at the Mötley members. Ozzy then goes on stage in fishnets and garters. Vince soon comes out on stage clanking in a knight's full suit of armour, to give Ozzy his drink: a cup full of flour in the face, before mooning the audience as he leaves the stage. The Crüe also gets even by walking on stage naked under Monks' clothes, flashing Ozzy and his band.

    With Mötley's popularity growing, Ozzy opts for the lamer Slade to open as support on his tour's second leg.

31/3/84

Shout At The Devil peaks on the US charts at number
seventeen, while Too Fast For Love also enjoys its highest
position at number seventy seven.

4/84

Randy Castillo plays drums on the second solo album titled
Dancin' On The Edge by Nikki's girlfriend, Lita Ford. He
joined the band after his roommate, who played in Lita's band,
called upon him to replace their fired drummer. On the tour
following its release, he is introduced to Nikki and Tommy at
Lita's Los Angeles concert, and they quickly become friends.

This month's issue of Record Review magazine features
Mötley Crüe on the cover for the first time in their career, and a
telephone interview with Nikki from Glen Falls, New York
before they played their second show with Ozzy.

24/4/84

The Crüe commences their three-week second headline tour in
Bakersfield, California with Saxon and Glasgow's Heavy Pettin'
in support, playing to audiences between 3,000 and 8,500.

30/4/84

In Colorado Springs, Colorado, Tommy runs down the fifth-
floor hallway of the Antlers Hotel in his leather g-string.
Spotted by an old lady, she calls the concierge to report the
indecent exposure and disturbance by a man with long black
hair, and hotel security then call the police. Upon arrival, the
cops find Mick in a state of undress in the men's restroom with
eighteen-year-old Heather Anderson. They are arrested at
3:45am and taken to El Paso County Jail, where they are soon
released on $50 bond. This is luck for Tommy, since he had
been convicted of disturbing the peace earlier in the year and
sentenced to two years' probation.

Too Young To Fall In Love is released as the second single
from Shout At The Devil and is again backed with a B-side
from their previous Too Fast For Love album; this time the

track chosen is Take Me To The Top. It peaks at number ninety and spends only two weeks on the U.S. charts. The oriental-themed video for the single is set during the 1920s in Shanghai, China. It is shot in an abandoned train tunnel under a 12th Avenue warehouse on the outskirts of Manhattan, New York, over thirty five hours using six sets and fifteen actors, running up a total production cost of seventy five thousand dollars. One of the actors is a young Michelle Yeoh, while a little boy named Billy acts in the clip by passing Nikki a note during a scene. The video is directed and produced by Martin Kahan, whose previous clips include Lick It Up by Kiss and Rock School by Heaven, both of whom Mötley has recently played shows with. Tommy phoned Nikki after seeing one of his video clips and said he wanted to work with this outrageous director for their next video.

15/5/84

Mötley plays the final show of their headlining tour in Memphis and celebrates by having Kevin Brady from Sunset Strip Tattoo join them on the road to ink the band's name on all of their upper left arms. In Evansville, Indiana two days earlier, Kevin tattooed a USDA Choice meat stamp on Vince Neil's left buttock. Tommy has a red rising sun with Japanese symbols for rhythm and power tattooed on his left shoulder.

The Crüe then heads out to begin playing another ten dates with Ozzy from tomorrow, including two festivals: the American Rock Festival held at Michigan's Timber Ridge Ski Area in Kalamazoo, and the Iowa Jam in Des Moines, Iowa in front of fifty two thousand punters with Accept, Night Ranger and Ted Nugent also on the bill. It's around this time that a Mötley Crüe vs. Quiet Riot war of words begins after their vocalist Kevin Dubrow says the Crüe sucks and wouldn't sell a record.

19/5/84

Before their show in Hollywood, Florida, Mötley holds an afternoon in-store at Peaches Records & Tapes in Fort Lauderdale.

20/5/84

Nikki's grandmother calls to let him know his Mum has had a heart attack and is in a very bad condition. He feels he should call her but feels he doesn't really know her, or care, since it's been ten years since he's had anything to do with her.

30/5/84

With a sell-out show in Syracuse, New York, Mötley kicks off a further thirteen headline shows, this time with their good friends in Ratt as support on seven of them, following release of their Out Of The Cellar debut album. Tommy previously appeared in Ratt's video for You Think You're Tough, and makes another appearance in their Back For More clip, this time with Nikki acting as policemen – they frisk drummer Bobby Blotzer up against the wall of the building at 8080 Melrose Ave. During the tour, Mötley develops a habit of biting everyone they like, often breaking the skin on people's arms.

15/6/84

The U.S. tour in support of Shout At The Devil ends in front of eight thousand people in Springfield, Massachusetts. After the tour, Vince and wife Beth move to 916 Esplanade, Redondo Beach into a two-bedroom apartment on the fourth-floor of the ten-story high-rise right on the beach front, not far from Mick and his girlfriend Linda Correia. Nikki soon moves in across the street from Mick with Robbin Crosby from Ratt, as his girlfriend Lita Ford goes on her own tour. His apartment only has one bed and Robbin lets Nikki sleep in it while he crashes on the floor. Nikki buys a new Corvette and makes out with other women. He soon hears that Lita is dating Mick Cocks from the band Heaven and formerly Rose Tattoo, after apparently being introduced by a local punk. Tommy and Nikki go to Lita's house and beat the punk with pieces of wood. Lita later calls Nikki and abuses him, also telling him they didn't meet through that punk.

4/7/84

With his friend Bob, a stoned Nikki fires a huge skyrocket out of his garden. It sets a forty-foot palm tree on fire that falls onto a 1965 Mustang convertible, sending it up in flames. Nikki thinks it's hilarious.

8/84

Nikki flies to Seattle to visit his sick mother who has recently been committed to a mental institution. It's the first time he has seen her since she put him on a Greyhound bus to his grandparents' home in Idaho six years ago. After asking if he wrote Looks That Kill about her, Nikki checks her out and takes her to his sister Ceci's place, before catching the next plane back to Los Angeles where he feels he belongs.

Around this time, Tommy's new champagne-coloured '82 Corvette runs over his foot as he urinates beside it.

18/8/84

The Crüe makes their first trip to the U.K. and plays the huge Monsters of Rock Festival in Donington at noon in front of about sixty thousand metalheads. The set comprises of songs Bastard, Ten Seconds To Love, Looks That Kill, Live Wire and Helter Skelter. After kicking off the show, Mötley is followed on stage by Y&T, Accept, Gary Moore, Ozzy Osbourne, Van Halen and AC/DC. A cow's eyeball is hurled at the band, amongst other animal parts, and it lodges in Tommy's drum riser. At the end of their set, Nikki throws his bass into the crowd and it lands on a fan named Stu Taylor, smashing his glasses and cutting his head open. A number of people take the guitar to the side of the stage to smash it up and share out the pieces.

25/8/84

The Crüe moves on with a lot of the bands on the Donington bill (Dio replaces Y&T after one show) to play six shows throughout Europe; the first in Stockholm, Sweden. Backstage at this show, Nikki lifts up Eddie Van Halen's shirt and bites him on the stomach, before Vince bites him on his hand, all much to the disgust of Eddie's wife, Valerie Bertinelli. At the Ritz hotel in Paris, France, a wasted Vince kicks in and shatters the glass entrance door as he tries to take a phone call.

2/9/84
Playing in Nuremburg, Germany, Mötley opens the show that in time turns out to be the last Van Halen performance with David Lee Roth singing. The mayhem continues afterwards as they get high in the hotel room of Dio's keyboardist Claude Schnell. While Claude leaves the room for a while, they throw his beds, chairs, desk, TV and dresser out of the window on top of two brand new Mercedes Benz cars parked below. On his return, he soon answers his door to German police with Rottweilers, before Dio's entire band is kicked out and banned for years. After the final show in Turin, Italy, Nikki travels to Paris where he spends a few days, before flying back to Los Angeles and meeting back up with the rest of the band.

9/84
Mötley Crüe begins recording demos of their new material for their third album, which is scheduled for release next January. A song title of Raise Your Hands To Rock is suggested by former Ozzy Osbourne drummer Carmine Appice. They also work on the previously demoed Nobody Knows What It's Like To Be Lonely.

27/9/84
The success of Shout At The Devil assists Mötley's debut album Too Fast For Love to achieve Gold status, now having sold five hundred thousand copies of the Elektra version in the U.S.
12/10/84

Mötley returns to London as they prepare to tour Europe in support of Iron Maiden on their Powerslave Tour. They attend the Iron Maiden party at Legends nightclub and photos of Vince and Tommy 'working' with female friends circulate quickly afterwards. Rehearsal venues include a kids' gymnasium in London, and a thirteenth century castle recommended by AC/DC. Nikki captures a lot of events at these rehearsals on his video camera, including footage of Mick poking his white butt out of a castle window.

15/10/84
The first of over twenty shows with Iron Maiden takes place in Cologne, Germany, before moving through Belgium, France, Denmark, Sweden, Finland, Italy and Switzerland. During the tour, practical jokes continue as members of Iron Maiden handcuff Vince to the stage so he can't sing, and they chant Alka Seltzer into the PA system during Helter Skelter. The Crüe then brings a table and chairs on stage during Iron Maiden's set, and sit down and enjoy a beer.

14/11/84
The final show of the Iron Maiden support tour takes place in Basel, Switzerland. Vince is so wasted that cortisone shots from doctors aren't helping him to sound any better on stage any more. In the hotel, Tommy and Vince let off a flare in their room after buying some flare guns. They run out of their room to get their manager Doc McGhee, to show him how funny it is that the flare landed on Tommy's mattress and set it on fire. On return, they realise they left their keys in the room. Smoke pours out the door and the sprinklers come on after a hotel worker finally opens it. They get kicked out of the hotel the following day, after breaking mirrors in the elevators.

19/11/84
As their last Shout At The Devil show, Mötley Crüe also plays their first U.K. headlining gig to wind up their European dates, in front of almost three thousand people at the Dominion

Theatre in London's West End, with Stratus in support. Nikki
wears a dark green one piece jester suit and paints his bass the
same colour. Vince trips on a monitor during the set and they
are generally disappointed with their performance. A new song
called Raise Your Hands To Rock is played live for the first
time. The English crowd again throws strange butcher meats at
the band during the songs, while Tommy pulls a dart from his
drum tech's back while he plays. The dry ice smoke machine
then blows up on his drum tech Clyde, whose face is badly
burnt from the scorching water. As they leave the stage,
Tommy moons the crowd with his bare butt for first time.

24/11/84

Tommy Lee Bass marries his girlfriend Candice—real name
Elaine Margaret Starchuk—after she says she wants to marry him
when he returns from the European tour. They open the
phonebook and pick a minister within minutes, before Tommy
picks out her wedding ring in downtown Los Angeles. At
seventeen years of age, Elaine Starchuk first arrived in L.A.
from her native Vancouver, Canada, and danced using the stage
name of Candice Starrek at The Body Shop on Sunset
Boulevard as well as other clubs. That same year, a couple of
her photos were published and led to a call from Penthouse to
do a shoot. Her marriage to Tommy lasts three months. Before
they were married, she found a photo of Tommy doing sexual
acts with two girls and in their first week of marriage, one of the
girls keeps calling their home phone number (that Tommy gave
them while he was drunk) and hanging up, causing the
newlyweds to argue. Convinced Tommy is having an affair, she
enters the kitchen where Tommy is making a peanut butter
sandwich, and tries to stab him with a butter knife grabbed
from the drawer but the knife doesn't go through. The final
straw comes after they go to a big World Wrestling Federation
event and head for the Tropicana afterwards to watch mud
wrestling. On the way in the limo with Vince, Beth, Roy
Thomas Baker and Tom Zutaut, Candice continues to rile
Tommy by calling his mum foul names, after she recently called

her Lisa, the name of Tommy's previous girlfriend. When she doesn't stop, Tommy loses restraint and punches her in the mouth knocking a temporary cap off her tooth. This is the first time Tommy ever hits a woman. She later claims Tommy forced her to abort their unborn child.

11/84
Mötley heads back to Los Angeles for a short break before recording their new album. In the meantime, a Helter Skelter picture disc begins pressing in the U.S., released with a huge poster and insert inside. Elektra is now giving Mötley the red carpet treatment and they plan to do big Christmas promotions and radio giveaways with the picture disc.

1/12/84
With his girlfriend, house and most of his friends gone after being on tour for over a year, Nikki decides to go on a Club Med holiday to the French-owned island of Martinique in the Caribbean, with Ratt's Robbin Crosby and photographer friend Neil Zlozower.

8/12/84
Vince is throwing a party at his apartment in Redondo Beach. Members of the Finnish band Hanoi Rocks end up partying with them for days, as they are on their month-long first U.S. tour, supporting their Two Steps From The Move album. A couple of girls with apartments in the complex also party with them, as well as Vince's neighbour Jim Thomas, who is an NBC anchorman.

    A couple of days into the party after taking some Quaaludes, and drinking Jack Daniels and a mix of Brandy and Kahlua, Mick has enough of the abuse dished out to him by his girlfriend Linda. He walks out of Vince's home onto the beach where he wades out into the water with his drink, intent on drowning himself to end it all before he blacks out. Vince later spots him washed up on the beach in his leather pants, jacket and boots, but Mick just wants to be left alone.

Vince asks his neighbour and car enthusiast Jim if he wants to drive his new red '72 Ford De Tomaso Pantera sports car to take him to the liquor store Redondo Food Mart at 529 S Catalina Ave so he can restock the party. Jim declines since him and his fiancée are heading off to a French restaurant in Malaga Cove. As he leaves, he introduces Jim to Razzle who says he'll go to the store with Vince instead.

Vince drives to the store with his passenger, twenty-four-year-old Hanoi Rocks drummer, Nicholas 'Razzle' Dingley, picking up a couple of hundred dollars-worth of beer and other alcohol, which Razzle holds in his lap during the ride back. At 6:38pm, just three to four blocks from his home 0.4 miles further ahead on the same street, Vince's car skids sideways for thirty-five feet, as it goes through a fifteen-feet wide wet spot of residential water run-off on the road. He loses control of the vehicle that's doing 65mph in a 25mph zone at the time. The car heads into oncoming traffic on the beachfront Esplanade northbound lane, and at three hundred and eleven feet north of Topaz St, in the block halfway between Sapphire St, it collides into the passenger's side of the only oncoming vehicle: a white '67 VW driven by eighteen-year-old Lisa Hogan, a resident of Rancho Palos Verdes. Her twenty-year-old passenger and boyfriend, Daniel Louis Smithers, is injured in the crash, as is Vince's friend Razzle, whose passenger side of the vehicle takes the crash impact. Vince is concussed and has cracked ribs and minor facial cuts when the ambulance arrives. When Tommy arrives at the scene on foot after hearing sirens go by Vince's house, he sees Vince sitting on the kerb with his head in his hands, and also sees Razzle's blue Converse sneaker in the middle of the road. Vince's blood alcohol level reads 0.17 when given a breathalyzer on the scene—well above the legal limit of 0.10. He is read his rights and taken by police in their squad car to the nearby city of Torrance, due to Redondo's jail being given its yearly painting.

Razzle is taken to Redondo's South Bay Hospital while Tommy drives his wife Candice, Vince's wife Beth and members of Hanoi Rocks there. After a long wait, a doctor advises them that Razzle died at 7:12pm, after his severe head injuries were too much.

Lisa Hogan is rushed in critical condition to the intensive care unit of Little Company of Mary Hospital in Torrance where she remains in a coma until the end of the month, with a broken arm and two broken legs. Her head injury leaves her liable to fly into psychomotor seizures as a result of some brain damage. Daniel Smithers is taken to South Bay Hospital suffering a broken leg and some brain damage. The driver of a third car involved, twenty-five-year-old Karimi Khaliabad of Torrance, is uninjured.

This date is ironically the first day of U.S.A. National Drunk Driving Awareness Week. The final five Hanoi Rocks shows in California and Arizona of the band's thirty-city U.S. Tour are cancelled, including what was to be their Los Angeles debut next Friday night.

9/12/84

Thinking he has drowned himself, Mick heads back to Vince's house from the beach, where he sees Tommy, Candice and Beth crying. He tries to walk through a glass door to hear them, thinking he is a ghost, but ends up flat on his back in the sand.

Vince is questioned about the accident by police, before they send him home as the sun comes up, where Beth and Tommy are waiting for him. Vince still has Razzle's blood on his Hawaiian shirt and shorts. Vince's phone runs hot with many calls from people asking what had happened. Manager Doc McGhee calls to tell him that the police have decided to arrest him for vehicular manslaughter, so he turns himself in to the precinct station where he is charged.

As Nikki enters Miami airport, returning from his holiday in Martinique, a fan wearing a blue blazer tells him that Vince has died in a car crash. Nikki calls Doc McGhee from a payphone and gets the full story.

The band's managers Doc McGhee and Doug Thaler were also on vacation at the time of the crash, and refuse to comment on the accident when contacted by their office. Staff members at Elektra Records are warned their jobs will be on the line if comments on the situation are made, due to the high possibility of lawsuits, should any damaging statements be made. Elektra decides to cancel the huge Helter Skelter picture disc promotional campaign and subsequently recalls the product from any further sales.

13/12/84

Vince is freed by posting $2,650 bail after being booked for investigation of driving under the influence and vehicular manslaughter.

28/12/84

Daniel Smithers is transferred from South Bay Hospital to a hospital in Ventura, California to be nearer his family. He attends rehabilitative therapy to learn how to speak all over again, as a result of his brain damage sustained. Ironically, he previously worked as a counselor at the Palmer Drug Abuse Program. Meanwhile sales of Mötley Crüe and Hanoi Rocks albums effectively double, as Vince grows a beard and continues to struggle to come to grips with what has happened.

1985

5/1/85

Following the cancellation of their U.S. tour, Hanoi Rocks plays two contracted gigs in Helsinki for a television broadcast on Europe-A-Go-Go, which they dedicate to the memory of their late drummer Razzle. Tommy Lee offers to play drums for them at the shows but it doesn't work out. Former drummer of The Clash, Terry (Tory) Chimes, plays the shows after rehearsing three or four times. With Vince Neil to face vehicular manslaughter charges in court in a few days, it is rumoured that Hanoi Rocks vocalist Michael Monroe will replace Vince in Mötley if he is jailed for a considerable period of time. Crüe manager Doug Thaler reports that members of both bands have been commiserating the loss, while jamming and collaborating on four or five songs; however Hanoi Rocks members Mike Monroe and Andy McCoy just sit around the house of Nikki Sixx and Robbin Crosby for days on end, shooting cocaine and heroin as their way of dealing with the tragedy.

9/1/85

Wearing a conservative grey suit, Vince attends South Bay Municipal Court in Torrance, California accompanied by his lawyer Michael Nasatir, a partner of Nasatir, Hirsch, Podberesky & Khero in Santa Monica. Vince hears the charges against him of vehicular manslaughter and drunk driving, which stem from his Dec. 8 car accident in Redondo Beach, in which his rock musician friend was killed and two people were injured. Vince stands silently during the two-minute arraignment, while his lawyer enters a plea of not guilty on his behalf. The judge allows Vince to remain free on two-and-a-half-thousand dollars bail pending a preliminary hearing in the case on February 20.

The trial is postponed many times throughout the year. Vince was previously found guilty of another drink-driving charge prior to the accident, meaning this time he could face up to seven years in jail, which places the future of Mötley Crüe in the balance. Newspaper headlines around the world call him a murderer. Returning from the preliminary hearing, Doc McGhee tells him that the court requires him to check into rehab. Vince spends thirty days of intense therapy with Bob Timmons in the Palmer Drug Abuse Program for rehabilitation at a detox hospital on Van Nuys Boulevard. He successfully completes the program but feels his career is over. Vince's parents and Beth visit him in rehab, but he doesn't see or hear from any of his band mates. Management offers Vince a twelve-thousand-dollar diamond and gold Rolex watch if he can last three months without a drink; an act they later strongly regret as it doesn't teach him his lesson.

2/85

Drinking more heavily than ever, Mick Mars discovers his BMW 320i has been taken from his Marina Del Ray apartment by his girlfriend Linda, as their relationship falls apart. She leaves Mick for a football player named Nick Frontero.

17/2/85

Mötley starts recording their next album with a title of Entertainment or Death at Cherokee with Tom Werman once again producing and Brad Gilderman as the engineer. Werman's charcoal-coloured Porsche sports a license plate of 33 RPM. The title and theme of the new album is inspired by Nikki's reading of Commedia dell'arte–a popular form of comedy employing improvised dialogue and masked characters that flourished in Italy from the sixteenth century to the eighteenth century. He also reads Antonin Artaud's essay titled Theatre Of Cruelty, which provides further inspiration. Nikki is intrigued by his learning that court jesters wearing motley-coloured clothing were beheaded if they failed to entertain the king. New theatrical stage outfits with more colourful, glittery, softer fabrics are designed and made by Australian Ray Brown, with the cost of their tour wardrobe totaling one-hundred-thousand dollars. Brown had recently made stage wear for Ozzy Osbourne, and the band visits his studio in LA's Playa Del Ray district where they exchange ideas and choose trashy glam-lace fabrics from his stock, and complete the look with rhinestone adornments.

Mötley enters the studio with only five songs that Nikki has written. Home Sweet Home is one of the first to be laid down and they want it to be their Dream On or Stairway to Heaven. After Tommy rehearses the song on a grand piano, producer Werman convinces him to record it on a small Roland keyboard in the studio instead. The Crüe gets up to all sorts of antics in the studio. Nikki tries to write while being high on drugs and trying to get two women to go down on each other. With his car license suspended, Vince gets around in chauffeur-driven limos and on his Harley Davidson motorbike.

6/3/85

At 4:10pm as Nikki and Vince make their way to the recording studio, a silver 1980 Cadillac Eldorado runs a stop sign as they turn onto Hollywood Boulevard, hitting Nikki's one-week-old jeep before taking off. Nikki and Vince abandon the jeep in the middle of the road and chase the driver. Nikki flags down a taxi as they run, having the taxi pull in front of the Cadillac after spotting it about eight cars ahead. Vince then jumps on top of the car and kicks in the windshield with his sneaker. The offender gets out and is detained by Vince while Nikki goes to a nearby gas station to call the police. Upon their arrival, they advise the Mötley men that they have been responsible for the capture of a man reputedly wanted by the Los Angeles Police Dept. for a number of hit-and-run accidents.

4/85

A wasted Tommy flips his motorbike seven times on a Los Angeles freeway with his Armored Saint bassist friend Joey Vera on the back, as he gives him a ride after seeing him play a show at a club in the mountains. Tommy escapes with minor injuries, while Joey's hand is mangled, taking him two months after surgery at County General Hospital before he can play again.

13/4/85

Vince's second child Elizabeth Ashley is born and named after her mother (but in later years she changes her name to Elle). This is the first child with his wife Beth Lynn. He has a young son Neil from a prior relationship with Tami Jones.

23/4/85

Nikki arrives back at the studio from a visit to Elektra's Mexican office, where he picks up a Most Popular Band in Mexico award for the band, as they even out sell Prince.

5/85

Mötley continues to record at Pasha and Record Plant West studios with Duane Baron engineering. The album is mixed at Record Plant West. Tommy records his drums at Pasha in four days with drums miked in one room and the amps in another, while Mick's guitar sounds are largely created at Cherokee.

Tommy receives notice that his marriage to Candice has been annulled, after they separated about a month ago. He then dates model Tawny Kitaen, who was the high school sweetheart of Ratt guitarist Robbin Crosby. Years later, Kitaen says, "With Tommy, he was constantly doing coke, so he wanted to go out. He just wore me out. I remember one night, we were lying on top of the bed and he took out two knives. He was trying to teach me how to throw a knife. 'You hold the top of the knife, and... boom!' By the end of the evening there must have been about 5,000 knife marks in the wall. That was his idea of a good time." Occasionally, Tommy still has sex with Candice while going out with Tawny.

6/85

A video for the first single of the new Mötley Crüe album is shot; a cover version of Smokin' In The Boys Room by Detroit band Brownsville Station, which went to number three on the charts for them in 1973. Mötley used to play the song during sound-checks and jams, and Vince suggests it be recorded for the album since he also enjoyed playing it in his previous band Rockandi. The Crüe's version features Willie Nelson's harmonica player Mickey Raphael. Producer Tom Werman loves it and feels it should be recorded ahead of a cover version of Mountain's classic Mississippi Queen. The video is shot in extreme summer heat at Woodland Hills High School in California's San Fernando Valley and is completed two days before the album's release. Actor Michael Berryman, who starred in the movies One Flew Over The Cuckoo's Nest and The Hills Have Eyes, acts as the Principal while the storyline centres around a schoolboy named Jimmy, played by Felix Montano. Mick befriends Michael Berryman, who was born with the condition Hypohidrotic Ectodermal Dysplasia that prevents the formation of hair, fingernails, teeth, and sweat glands.

A single titled Stars is released from the Hear 'N Aid project that Vince and Mick contribute to. Dio bassist Jimmy Bain, who organises the project, phoned Vince to ask if they wanted to participate. The album, featuring many of today's hard rock giants, is recorded to help raise money for starving Africans. Set to sing a solo part on the song, Vince is unable to due to a scheduling conflict as Mötley Crüe shoots their new video the same day that he's required in the studio.

Tommy and Bobby Blotzer from Ratt call Lita Ford's former drummer Randy Castillo from a party they're at with Ozzy Osbourne, and tell him that Ozzy needs a new drummer. Randy has recently broken his right leg in a skiing mishap in his home state of New Mexico, but catches a plane the next day to audition—cast, crutches and all. The audition doesn't go as planned due to the broken leg but a friendship is cemented.

21/6/85

Mötley Crüe's third album titled Theatre of Pain is released and debuts on the charts at number ninety, at a cost of almost $200,000 to produce. (Manager Doug Thaler got the previous

Entertainment or Death album title tattooed on his arm a week before the band decided to change the name to Theatre of Pain.) The album cover is illustrated by Dave Willardson and shows two drama masks, one bearing a pentagram. The concept was developed by Nikki with Bob Defrin, who also designed the new Mötley Crüe logo. Included on the album is the song Louder Than Hell that was demoed for Shout At The Devil when it was called Hotter Than Hell. It changes as the band feels 'louder' is what they are about more. The track Tonight (We Need A Lover) also seems to have been created from the unreleased Shout demo track called Black Widow, which is supposed to end up on a movie soundtrack with Mike Monroe from Hanoi Rocks on vocals, collaborated with Gene Simmons. Save Our Souls is penned from some reworked verses of the unreleased Running Wild In the Night, since there was a lack of fresh material for the album.

24/6/85

Smokin' In The Boys Room is released in the U.S. as the first single from Theatre of Pain. It becomes Mötley Crüe's first Top 40 single, peaking at number sixteen and spending fifteen weeks on the U.S. charts. Use It Or Lose It is included on the B-side of the single.

7/7/85

The Theatre of Pain tour kicks off at the Sun Plaza in Tokyo, Japan; the Crüe's first show in the land of the rising sun. The tour begins with five concerts in Tokyo (the first four sell-outs), followed by Nagoya and Osaka. Mick switches from using Gibson guitars to Kramer, utilising Kramer Explorers, Barettas, and Pacers. Vince and Tommy get mobbed by fans in a McDonalds restaurant and are assisted by Tokyo Police. Nikki remains in his room where he suffers from having no heroin. He realises that he has become a junkie, whilst his band-mates are unaware of how much he has been scoring and shooting up.

15/7/85

The short Japanese tour concludes in Osaka and the Crüe returns to the United States. They prepare to embark on a headlining U.S. tour in two weeks, featuring a huge amount of lights and a ninety-degree tilting drum riser for Tommy's drum solo. Eddie Van Halen's guitar technician Rudy Leiren replaces Mark Mulcahy as the tech for Mick.

Tommy soon meets actress star of Dynasty and TJ Hooker, Heather Locklear, backstage at an REO Speedwagon show at the L.A. Forum. They are introduced by Mötley's accountant Chuck Shapiro, who is also REO Speedwagon's accountant, and they briefly chat. Tommy then chases her phone number down the following week from Chuck's brother, who is Heather's dentist. He calls her while watching The Fall Guy and tells her that he is watching her on TV. She turns on her TV and tells him that it's Heather Thomas. They talk for hours, before they set up a date for the following Friday night. Tommy picks her up from her Tudor-style house in the Tarzana hills where she lives with one of her three older sisters and they go out for their first date-dinner at an Italian Restaurant and the late show at The Comedy Club. During the night she tells him she has been out with a lot of rich guys in the past, as well as actor Scott Baio, and Tommy feels she is a good girl longing for a bad boy, but he plays it carefully. She also has a Mötley cassette tape in her car. For their second date, Tommy visits her home during the day and they swim, dance and drink lots of champagne with Heather's sister. They start spending more time together going out to dinner, parties and movies. Heather was raised in suburban Thousand Oaks as the youngest of four children.

17/7/85

Theatre of Pain is released in Australia, while Vince performs Smokin' In The Boys Room at the Farm Aid II benefit concert with Jon Bon Jovi, Willy Nelson and others.

31/7/85

Mötley Crüe's Theatre of Pain U.S. tour begins at the Glens Falls Civic Center in upstate New York with Y&T in support. The album currently sits in the Top 20 of the Billboard album chart. They travel from show to show in a private plane, painted black with a giant penis and testicles emblazoned on the tail.

2/8/85

Playing the second show of their U.S. tour in New Haven, Connecticut, the Crüe is joined on stage by former Brownsville Station member Cub Koda for a jam on guitar and vocals to Smokin' In The Boys Room, the song he wrote in 1973. Whenever they play the song live, the harmonica solo is played backstage by their tour security guy Fred Saunders. Since Vince can't play the instrument, he just pretends to play it live on stage.

3/8/85

Mötley plays an outdoor show at the Manning Bowl football stadium in Lynn, Massachusetts before fifteen thousand people, billed as Summer Jam '85. Originally scheduled for Kingston, NH, the concert was moved because the anticipated crowd numbers couldn't be handled. Twenty-five-year-old Alfred Reice of Flushing, New York is arrested outside the grounds for selling false documents and larceny, when he is caught with forty counterfeit tickets on him. An audience member is taken to hospital with suspected broken ribs after being crushed against a metal barrier by the crowd. Although the show is meant to start at 1pm, it doesn't begin until 2.40 due to the late arrival of some of Mötley Crüe's equipment from their previous concert. As a result, Helix doesn't perform, so Y&T open and are followed by Accept.

4/8/85

Onstage in Providence, Rhode Island, a fan grabs Vince's scarf and pulls him into the audience. When he is pulled back on stage by security, he realises his pants have been entirely ripped off, causing him to run backstage wearing just his boots. He returns in Tommy's stage underwear to finish the concert.

7/8/85

Tickets for the front row seats of Mötley's concert at Civic Arena in Pittsburgh are donated to Abraxas, a local treatment program for drug and alcohol abuse. These are auctioned off for over $1,000. Vince also records a series of public service announcements for Abraxas. Meanwhile the Crüe's own drug usage gets to the point where they shoot heroin on stage. They also mainline Jack Daniels and gin at night, shooting it up rather than drinking it, to come down off their cocaine. They also drink and do drugs in front of Vince and chew him out if they catch him having one drink, warning him of his pending trial and the consequences of being seen drinking. Vince turns to women as his new vice of choice, going through four or five most nights.

14/8/85

Before the show at New York City's Madison Square Gardens, the crowd is so psyched to see Mötley that during the set from Japanese support band Loudness, fireworks are tossed amongst the crowd. The venue's announcer tells the crowd that the fireworks have to stop or the band will not perform. After the show, Nikki goes to Alphabet City and scores some heroin before returning to the hotel and hanging out with Eddie Ojeda from Twisted Sister and a girl.

17/8/85

Theatre of Pain continues to climb the U.S. charts and peaks at number six, the highest position of any Mötley album to date.

19/8/85

In an interview leading up to Mötley's concert at Five Seasons Center in Cedar Rapids Iowa, Nikki says the band is trying to gain Guinness Book of Records' recognition as the loudest band in the world. After reading the comments, city officials issue earplugs and earmuffs to employees and security officers working at the concert. An employee Safety Director from the City of Cedar Rapids uses a noise meter to monitor the sound levels. The average reading during the band's ninety-minute set is 108 to 110 decibels, with an average reported level of 116 decibels for people standing close to the stage in front of the speaker columns. At one point, thirteen to fifteen pyrotechnic explosions in the performance push the meter to 127 decibels. People begin to feel physical pain at about 125 decibels. There's no doubting that Mötley certainly is Louder Than Hell.

24/8/85
Proceeds of Mötley Crüe's Los Angeles show are donated to the Encino-based Palmer Drug Abuse Program, where one of Vince's car crash victims once worked. The band treats Vince as somewhat of an outsider on tour, due to his upcoming trial.

After handing out flyers for their band before the concert, Poison's Bret Michaels and CC Deville are taken backstage by Nikki and invited on stage to perform the encore medley; it's their first time on a big stage.

8/85
An authorised biography written by Dante Bonutto called The Comedy and the Tragedy is published, as the official Crüe fan club S.I.N. (Safety in Numbers) continues to grow in membership, making it one of the largest fan clubs in the U.S.

Vince works hard towards gaining a black belt in the Tang Soo Do style of karate, while Mick's computer is stolen, losing the war game he was programming.

Tommy shows Polaroid photos of naked Heather to his band-mates at rehearsals. He watches dirt bike racing with her on TV one day and comments that he'd like to try it; the next day he finds a new dirt bike outside his house from her. He feels he wants to be with her for a long, long time.

Guitarist and singer John Corabi moves to Los Angeles from Philadelphia with his wife Valerie and her nine-year-old daughter, after loving the place when he visited six months earlier on an anniversary trip. John got his first tattoo a couple of years earlier: the words 'John & Valerie' on his arm. After playing in a heap of cover bands on the circuit in the Philly-New Jersey-Delaware area for a few years, he started doing some originals but found there wasn't really a market for it. The rest of his band called Angora soon follows him to L.A., encouraged by winning recent awards for Best New Band in their local club scene. Angora soon falls apart due to drug and social problems. At one point, Gene Simmons from Kiss looks to sign Angora, but wants to change their name to 8-BALL because the guys in the band have eight balls (testicles) collectively.

1/9/85
Theatre of Pain and Shout At The Devil both reach double-Platinum status.

20/9/85
Vince flies back to Los Angeles in between Crüe concerts in Ohio to meet with Deputy District Attorney Roger Kelly and the families of his accident's victims in court. As part of a plea bargain, his lawyer advises him to plead guilty to his vehicular manslaughter charge, to avoid the matter going to trial. His lawyer uses the angle that since most of the members at the party were from Mötley Crüe and Hanoi Rocks, it can be construed that it was a business meeting, and therefore the band's limited liability insurance could cover the payment of much higher damages to the victims, than if Vince were to have to pay them himself. The families agree and Torrance Superior Court Judge Edward A. Hinz Jr. sentences Vince to thirty days in County Jail to be served at the end of his Theatre of Pain world tour in the middle of next year, plus five years' probation, and completion of two hundred hours of community service. He also orders restitution of $1.8 million to be paid to Lisa Hogan, who was critically injured and spent weeks in a coma after the accident. The other victim Daniel Smithers shall receive $700,000, while $200,000 will go to the estate of

Nicholas "Razzle" Dingley, who died in the crash. The District Attorney's office says Vince has already performed forty to fifty hours of community service, including last month's Mötley Crüe concert at the Forum in Inglewood, which benefited the Palmer Drug Abuse Program, where Daniel Smithers was a program counselor. Many believe he has received a lenient penalty, due to his lawyer's plea bargaining to buy his way out of jail. Newspaper headlines now read, "Drunk Killer Vince Neil Sentenced to Touring World with Rock Band" causing bittersweet feelings inside Vince.

24/9/85
Tommy calls Heather from Bloomington, Indiana during a day off and holds the phone next to his left forearm. Heather hears the hum of a tattoo needle as it etches a big black rose ribboned with Heather's name into Tommy.

27/9/85
As Mötley plays Shout at the Devil during their concert at Von Braun Civic Center in Huntsville, Alabama, thirteen-year-old audience member Robby Miller is struck in the eye by an object, believed to be dry-ice propelled from the band's smoke effects on stage. Blood also splatters from his lip, covering the shirt he is wearing in blood.

2/10/85
Heather Locklear proposes to Tommy in their Dallas, Texas hotel room. He is incredulous and tells her to not say that kind of stuff unless she means it, as he doesn't want to be heartbroken.

3/10/85
Mötley's Tour Manager Rich Fisher is an avid golfer and Vince joins him for a round on the course at their hotel TPC Four Seasons Las Colinas near Dallas Fort Worth Airport. Enjoying his first-ever game of golf on their day off, Vince rents some

clubs, but buys his first set upon returning to the clubhouse and pro-shop.

6/10/85

After their San Antonio, Texas show, Mötley Crüe donates $17,500 to ALL-STAR, a non profit youth peer leadership organisation that Vince has been working with to educate students in becoming responsible drivers. Vince gives anti-drink-driving talks at schools. Front row seats for their upcoming shows in Rochester and Pittsburgh are auctioned by a radio station, raising $1,000 for an alcohol and drug education program.

Vince tears ligaments in his knee while water-skiing in Texas, which causes him to wear a brace on his knee under his stage clothes, and forces him to give up his karate lessons. He finishes at red belt, one before his black belt goal.

26/10/85

Home Sweet Home is released as the second single from Theatre of Pain, and is backed with Red Hot from the Shout At The Devil album. The single peaks at number eighty nine and spends only six weeks in the charts. Nikki wrote some of the lyrics for the song when he was seventeen years old. Playing the song live on tour night after night, Tommy feels he wants to make his own home with Heather.

31/10/83

Mötley appears live on MTV for the first time during their Halloween Horror Show with live footage from the Crüe's show at the Limelight Club in New York being broadcast to millions of viewers. MTV also runs a Crüe Halloween contest, where the winner Debbie McIntosh from Ohio and twenty-five friends are flown in for the private show, plus the following night's concert in Chicago, taking up the entire front row.

11/85

The video for the band's latest single Home Sweet Home first airs, having been made in Texas the previous month. Much of the footage for the video was filmed in Houston and Amarillo, with the audience and venue shots being filmed in Dallas. The night before the Dallas shoot, Nikki freaks out after having an eight-ball of cocaine and four blue pills. He has visions of his mother and father and starts tearing his hair out while standing on top of a table, before convulsing with a foaming mouth. On the set the next day, his bass tech Tim Luzzi sees Nikki talking with an imaginary friend under the stage before the video shoot begins. The video becomes MTV's most requested clip for the next four months, prompting MTV to change its request line rules and establish an expiration date for new videos to stop requests continually coming in. It's also MTV's first power ballad aired.

A US Senate committee on pornography in rock music condemns Mötley Crüe's lyrics for degrading women and glorifying violence. So in the middle of the tour, a concept for the next stage show is first brought up. Sitting around wasted on the tour bus, they come up with the idea of having a huge backdrop of a spread-legged female, and the band could enter the stage through the middle of her legs.

The Dead Milkmen scores a college radio hit with their song Bitchin' Camaro on their Big Lizard in My Backyard debut album. The comedy punk rock song includes the lyric, "Don't forget to get your Mötley Crüe t-shirt, y'know, all proceeds go to get their lead singer out of jail." Other Crüe-related music released this year includes Tommy's contribution on Espionage's second album titled ESP on Elektra Records and produced by Roy Thomas Baker, as well as Tommy and Vince making a guest appearance on Night Ranger's third album titled 7 Wishes.

19/12/85

Manager Doc McGhee becomes so tired of trying to keep Vince sober while on probation, he leaves him in his Orlando,

Florida hotel room with two security guys instructed to beat him up.

21/12/85

Mötley's successful U.S. tour ends in Florida. A pedometer shows Tommy averages twelve miles each night on the drums. Tommy looks like a criminal in his new passport photo, after stacking a friend's Honda motocross bike in a ditch, wearing no helmet. Vince heads to the Cayman Islands for a few days' holiday before the European tour commences early next year. He meets up with Jon Bon Jovi and Pat Travers there and they jam every night at the local pub. Nikki returns to Los Angeles after the tour. His yuppie, actress-in-practice girlfriend and drug-buddy Nicole, who he met through the band's lawyer as an attempt to clean Nikki up somewhat, meets him at the airport with syringes and they party their night away shooting heroin.

24/12/85

On Christmas Eve, Tommy formally proposes to his actress girlfriend Heather Locklear, while riding in a limousine along the Ventura Freeway with their heads in the wind outside the open moon-roof. With eyes watering and his hair flapping in his face, Tommy placed a 2.3-carat diamond ring on her finger and yells, "Will you marry me?" "Yes!" she shouts back.

25/12/85

Nikki spends Christmas morning with a girl he picked up at a strip club the night before, before taking her home on his Harley and later having Christmas dinner by himself in McDonalds.

1986

18/1/86
Mötley Crüe holds a press conference called New Year's Evil at Frankenstein Castle near Frankfurt to promote their first European tour. The event doubles as a meet and greet for fifty German competition winners and fifty American soldiers stationed in Germany.

22/1/86
Mötley's first European headlining tour gets underway, with Cheap Trick as special guests on nine U.K. dates. The bands jam together on stage to the AC/DC classic Highway to Hell.

14/2/86
Mötley plays the first of two concerts at London's Hammersmith Odeon on Valentine's Day and the guys from Hanoi Rocks watch the performance, as does Brian Connolly from the Sweet. After the show, Nikki Sixx grabs a taxi with Andy McCoy from Hanoi Rocks in search of scoring some heroin. They find a dealer on the street that shoots Nikki up inside a house, as he is already feeling too wasted to inject. Nikki passes out while Andy tries to wake him up by putting ice in his pants, followed by the dealer attempting to revive him by hitting him all over with a baseball bat. When that doesn't work, the dealer carries him outside on his shoulder to throw him into a trash dumpster. Nikki vomits on his shoes and comes back to life.

16/2/86
Cheap Trick's Rick Nielson introduces Tommy Lee and Nikki to one of Tommy's favourite drummers, Roger Taylor of Queen. Roger takes them and Cheap Trick singer Robin Zander to a Russian restaurant in London where they drink infused vodka and dine. As seven large lines of cocaine are presented to

the guests on silver platters for desert, Nikki snorts them all. Back at their hotel bar, Nikki urinates on Rick Nielson's black rubber coat.

6/3/86
Mötley completes their European tour in France. On their days off, the band and crew often played golf, went go-kart racing or ten-pin bowling – promoters would hire out the entire bowling alley for their exclusive use. During the last show in Paris, Warren DeMartini from Ratt and Phil Collen from Def Leppard jam with the Crüe on stage. French TV show footage from the concert includes Nikki exposing himself as they enter the backstage area after the show.

13/3/86
Vince Neil announces Mötley Crüe's participation in Live Aid II during a press conference at the Biltmore Hotel in Los Angeles. They don't end up playing at the concert though.

4/86
Back in Los Angeles, Nikki meets his girlfriend Nicole who picked out a house for Nikki to buy while he was on tour. She shows him around the house at 14432 Valley Vista Boulevard in Sherman Oaks and he hardly leaves; shooting up to $1,000 worth of drugs a day with her as his veins start to collapse and dry out. Izzy Stradlin' from Guns N' Roses often comes over, as does Britt Eckland and various porn stars, until paranoia sets into Nikki and he becomes a recluse. He often patrols his house for intruders with his .357 magnum and pulls his loaded gun on employees of his home security provider West Tech Security. The single-level home was built in 1940 and has three bedrooms and two bathrooms in the contained 2,289 sqft on a 0.34 acre lot. The house is interior decorated with red velvet hangings, gothic furniture, antiques and gargoyles that loom at you out of the darkness.

10/5/86

Tommy's second marriage begins as he marries TV star Heather Locklear in the palmy courtyard of the Santa Barbara Biltmore hotel bedecked with gardenias and tulips. Heather currently acts as Sammy Jo in Dynasty and cop Stacey Sheridan in TJ Hooker. Tommy wears a white leather tuxedo made by Mötley's stage clothing designer Ray Brown, while Heather wears a skintight white strapless mermaid-style dress. The nondenominational forty-minute ceremony takes place in front of five hundred guests. Nikki is Tommy's best man but he lets him down as he is too wasted on heroin to fulfill his duties properly, even shooting up in the bathroom with syringes he hides in his cowboy boots. Skydivers drop in to the lavish ceremony carrying magnums of Cristal champagne. Once pronounced, twelve white doves are released, following a lengthy kiss. Guests include members of Ratt, Autograph, Quiet Riot, and Night Ranger, while Rikki Rachtman is the DJ for the event. Prenuptial revels included a lingerie-and-sex-toy shower for Heather and a bachelor party with fifteen bikinied mud wrestlers for Tommy.

The couple honeymoons on Grand Cayman Island for three weeks, and police are soon called when a late-night fight breaks out between the newlyweds at the luxurious Colonial Club. Tommy shouts obscenities, while glasses smash and furniture gets overturned as the couple argues for over half-an-hour to the sounds of someone getting slapped. Residents outside their third-floor room tell them to be quiet and are soon faced with Tommy challenging them, before threatening to kill Heather. A police car turns up and asks Heather if she wants to press charges but she says no. The fight continues inside their room until two more police cars arrive with five officers. The holiday club soon throws them out of their hotel for the disturbance.

Nikki spends the wedding weekend at the Biltmore Hotel in Santa Barbara with Nicole, determined to give up drugs, to no avail. Trying to come up with a way to kick drugs without going to rehab, he decides that he and Nicole should detox for five days at Doc McGhee's home. His manager later says, "Those five days felt like a year. Nikki was just so sick – I had to keep carrying him from the house to the hot tub because he was cramping up so bad."

11/5/86
Nikki receives a letter from Mötley Crüe's accountant explaining that he's been spending $3,500 per day on drugs and in sixteen months he will be broke, if not dead.

5/86
After not responding to his accountant's letter, Nikki is intervened on by band management and rehab specialist, Bob Timmons, as he and girlfriend Nicole agree to check into the same detox hospital on Van Nuys Boulevard that Vince went to last year. Nikki escapes after three days when they try and brainwash him with religion. Bob Timmons says he will work with Nikki using other methods to get him clean. When Nicole comes home after another two weeks in rehab, they find they are not compatible now they are trying to live sober, so they break up.

Nikki writes an ode to his sick grandmother Nona for the soundtrack to the film Out of Bounds. It remains incomplete when Nikki begins his heroin detox program. With Tommy also on his honeymoon at the time, Nikki prefers not to use studio musicians on the track.

A six-foot-six personal assistant named Billy Kid moves in with Nikki to help keep him sober but it doesn't take long before they are drinking and shooting cocaine together. They pick girls out on their TV and imagine different dating scenarios. One day Nikki sees the video for the song Nasty Girl by Vanity 6 and he has his management company hook him up with the singer–Prince protégé and actress, Vanity. Her band was originally called Hookers and she played a hooker on stage wearing underwear. A week later he heads to her Beverly Hills apartment for his first date and when she opens the door naked they are soon a couple and freebase cocaine together. She was born Denise Katrina Matthews on 4 January 1959 in Niagara Falls, Ontario, Canada to a German mother and African-American father.

6/86

Nikki writes music for the film Never Too Young To Die with Gene Simmons from Kiss, including the title track and a song called Boom Boom Boom Goes The Beat Of My Heart. Nikki's new girlfriend Vanity stars in the movie with Gene Simmons. Nikki also writes the lyrics to a song Girls, Girls, Girls that Gene says are too radical and won't get played on the radio, so Nikki pulls all the songs and keeps them for work on the next Mötley album.

14/6/86

Vince moves into a $1.5 million house in the Porter Ranch estate in upper Northridge with his wife Beth and young daughter Elizabeth, as he prepares to turn himself into authorities to start his jail sentence. Vince wants to make sure his wife and daughter are safe and well taken care of.

15/6/86

Vince enters Gardena City Jail to fulfill his thirty-day jail sentence. Immediately granted the privileged position of a trustee, he works by delivering food to inmates, cleaning cells and washing police cars to earn time off his sentence as credit. Vince shares his prison cell with two guys, one who was inside for stealing exotic sports cars like Ferraris and Porches. After spending months on the road trying to stay sober, the prison guards reward his good behaviour with privileges of burgers and six-packs of beer. He signs many autographs and has photos taken with the guards, and is even allowed to take a female fan visitor into his cell for an hour one day, where they have sex. Beth only visits him every day for the first week.

1/7/86

Vince is released from jail, having his sentence reduced to eighteen days for good behaviour. Unable to contact his wife, his AA sponsor friend Keith picks him up from prison and they drive around Northridge for an hour looking for his new house, since he'd only slept there one night after moving in. After finding it, he breaks in through the back door and sees that Beth has left him, taking everything in the house except for his gold Rolex and his new 1983 model red Chevrolet Camaro Z28 car (although she did take its keys).

15/7/86

Nikki's grandfather calls to tell him that his grandmother Nona has passed away. He gives directions for him to attend her funeral the following Saturday, to which Nikki promises, but his drug problem prevents him from attending. He also avoids having to confront his past, confront his mother and spend time with his family, whom he ran away from as a teenager; they had abandoned him and he had abandoned them. He shoots some cocaine and watches Gilligan's Island on TV instead, feeling immense feelings of guilt but being too wasted to face his reality. He had a very close relationship with her, as she virtually brought him up when he was a child, and Nikki often has nightmares for many years following this day, about not being there for his grandparents at this time.

20/7/86

The day following his grandmother's funeral, Nikki resolves to clean up his act so he can write for the Mötley album. He finishes his ode called Nona and plays it to his friend and former Mötley A&R man Tom Zutaut, who is now at Geffen Records, recently signing a new band called Guns N' Roses. He loves the tune, and asks Nikki if he can produce the debut album for Guns N' Roses. After much goading from Zutaut, he eventually declines as he has his hands full trying to reduce his level of drug intake, but it encourages Nikki with his own song writing.

22/8/86

Mötley performs at an all-star jam at The Roxy in Los Angeles, along with members of Autograph, Kiss, Dio and King Kobra. They jam on Smokin' In The Boys Room, Highway To Hell and Jailhouse Rock.

8/86

Filming finishes for a forthcoming Mötley Crüe home-video, as Tommy tears the ligaments on both sides of his ankle when he goes over backwards on his dirt bike doing a wheelie out the front of his house. After having his leg in a cast for some time, he cuts it off at the beach with a steak knife.

Vince has a mud pit installed next to his swimming pool for female wrestling entertainment. He hosts many parties, often bringing back a dozen girls from the Tropicana strip club to wrestle nude for him and his friends. The most vicious fighter of the mud wrestlers is a girl named Sharise, who always wins the bouts. Randy Castillo frequents Vince's place, after being introduced to him by a drug dealer attending many of the parties.

Ozzy Osborne phones Randy and asks him to join his band on the spot, since his broken leg has now fully recovered. Randy flies to Scotland the next day and joins Ozzy's band. Later that day, he gets a call from Steve Vai asking him to join David Lee Roth's solo band and another call from David Coverdale asking if he would be interested in joining Whitesnake.

5/9/86

At the MTV Video Music Awards held at Universal Amphitheatre in Los Angeles, Tommy and Vince present the Most Experimental Video award on stage, which is won by a-ha for their Take on Me video - the night's biggest winner overall. Tommy and Vince both wear animal print suits made by the Crüe's clothing designer Ray Brown.

9/86

Mötley signs a new deal with Elektra Records for a minimum of six albums.

10/86

The Crüe is back in the studio working on the next album with Tom Werman, due to be released next January. Songs are being recorded at One to One, Rumbo Recorders and Conway Recording Studios, but Nikki finds himself shooting heroin again, as well as freebasing cocaine. He also gets hooked on methadone when he tries to withdraw, which considerably slows the writing and recording process of the album.

During the recordings, Tommy reinforces the ambient kick sound of his drums with a more open, sub-sonic kick from a sample. It's the first sample used in the band's music.

11/86

Vince is offered the role of the Prince in a rock musical version of Cinderella, but declines due to a conflict with the tour scheduling for next year. He also turned down a cameo role as a security guard in the movie Trick Or Treat earlier in the year.

Vince has Kevin Brady tattoo him a design of a naked woman kneeling on a bed of skulls on his forearm with a banner underneath reading Girls, Girls, Girls to show his preference for the title of the new album. Tommy has a very large tattoo of a peacock sitting on a bonsai tree inked on his right upper leg. It's his second tattoo on his right leg, as he already has a grinning devil drinking a Budweiser beer and holding a pitch fork on his ankle. Vince has a tattoo of Thumper the rabbit on his right ankle which was inked by Robert Benedetti, while Nikki sports a banner with a girl's name on his right ankle.

A forty-four-minute home-video called Uncensored is released, which includes videos clips and interviews with the band. One scene shows Vince living it up on Sunset Boulevard in a $1,000-per-day limo with girls lifting their tops, as the song Breakout by Shooting Star plays in the background. Rare live footage of the Take Me To The Top and Public Enemy #1 videos being watched by the Crüe at Cherokee Studios is also included. Other footage shows Nikki getting a chest tattoo at Sunset Strip Tattoos, Mick driving his red 1976 Chevrolet Corvette L82 from his Redondo Beach apartment, and Tommy riding his Harley Davidson bike around Hollywood. The video is directed by Wayne Isham with Robin Sloan being the Executive Producer of the project.

12/86

Nikki co-writes a song called Falling In and Out Of Love with his former girlfriend Lita Ford for her self-titled album. Working in the studio next to her, Lita comes in one day and they sit at a piano together and start playing and humming the tune. Nikki snorts drugs off the piano as they try to write. Lita is shocked at how much Nikki has let himself go but she doesn't say anything to him about his state.

25/12/86

Spending his Christmas Day alone in his mansion near Van Nuys, Nikki crouches naked under his Christmas tree with a needle in his arm. He often spends time high in his bedroom closet surrounded by his drug paraphernalia and guns, convinced that people are in his house and coming to get him. He is often too scared to move from this refuge until he comes down with heroin, usually scored from his dealer Jason.

31/12/86

Nikki's girlfriend Vanity comes over to his home and they take drugs all day before arguing. Nikki kicks her out and ends up in his closet with his grandfather's gun pointed at the door.

1987

early 87

Vince Neil appears with Ozzy Osbourne in Autograph's video for their song Loud and Clear, the title track of their third album. Vince and Tommy cameo as horn players in the Night Ranger video for The Secret of My Success, and also play in a golf tournament sponsored by Night Ranger.

12/1/87

As Mötley Crüe enters the studio to begin recording their next album, Nikki Sixx enrolls in a methadone program recommended by one of his childhood heroes. His weight soon drops to 164 pounds; 40 pounds less than a year ago.

30/1/87

Lying around his house all day, naked, Nikki writes a new song called Wild Side; a raped and dismantled version of the Lord's Prayer. However, he generally struggles to write any good songs. One day he brings a song to the studio called Hollywood Nights that is so bad, it's unusable.

19/2/87

Nikki buys a book written in 1937 by Bernard Falk called Five Years Dead that inspires a song of the same name and gets his creative juices flowing more. He also buys an old coffin.

3/3/87

Nikki writes an unused song in open tuning called Veins.

7/3/87

The songs Dancing On Glass and You're All I Need are written in the studio when material for the next Mötley album runs short. Nikki writes You're All I Need for his ex-girlfriend Nicole. He believes she cheated on him while he was on tour last year by seeing General Hospital actor Jack Wagner, whose 1985 song All I Need topped the Billboard Adult Contemporary chart. Nikki's lyrics of the Crüe song are about killing your girlfriend, so he takes a copy on cassette to her home and plays it to her. She calls him an asshole and Nikki phones some bikers to break Wagner's kneecaps.

Nikki is persuaded to have his ode titled Nona included on the album. With recording finally complete, all the tracks are mixed at Conway Recording Studios in Los Angeles.

13/3/87
Wearing a new jacket with a Nazi armband, Nikki enjoys a night out at the Cathouse in Hollywood, where he shoots up in the VIP bathroom.

24/3/87
Having completed the recording of their new album, Tommy and Nikki fly first class to New York for a week to oversee the album's mastering process.

2/4/87
Nikki and Tommy go on a fishing trip with their engineer Duane Baron. High on cocaine out on the lake, they hallucinate and play the mastered Girls album over and over on Tommy's little ghetto blaster. Their manager Doc meets them and tells them that Jon Bon Jovi thinks they've written the greatest song of their career in You're All I Need.

Vince frequents Palm Springs and the Caribbean to keep amused while not touring. He also spends time on the road with Bon Jovi for a few days in Atlanta, singing with them on encore jams and hanging out in a local strip joint called Tattletales. Tommy continues to ride his dirt bike, as well as regularly tearing up Californian golf courses. Mick spends much of his time buying guns.

10/4/87

West Tech Security sends a guard to Nikki's home, only to find him naked and waving a shotgun, accusing the guard of bugging his house. Doc McGhee smoothes the situation over but is tired of Nikki's out of control drug paranoia – he sees Mexicans and midgets running round his house, he sets alarms off, or is seen by neighbours crawling naked around his garden with a shotgun at least twice a week.

13/4/87

Mötley shoots their video for Girls, Girls, Girls with director Wayne Isham. With a strip club theme planned for the video, they originally want to use The Body Shop but since that venue is all-nude and doesn't serve alcohol, they end up shooting it at The Seventh Veil instead. By the time they finish at the club, none of them are functioning properly. They leave the club in a few cars to go to Wayne's studio nearby to film inserts, stopping off at a Mexican restaurant for shooters on the way.

15/4/87

As a drugged-up Nikki lies on his bed at home with Vanity, he hears voices and people moving about his house. He starts shouting and fires his .357 through his bedroom door at them. After barricading themselves in the bedroom overnight, he later realises it was just his radio and he shot a hollow point right through his new JBL speakers. As Vanity leaves the house the following day, she tells Nikki they are soul mates and asks him to marry her. Not wanting to face her going crazy and starting another argument, he says yes but feels his funeral will come before their wedding anyway.

19/4/87

Nikki meets Andy McCoy at a club but wants to leave soon after. They head back to Nikki's place where he shows a sober Andy his closet and encourages him to get high. Andy tells Nikki that he has a habit and leaves. Nikki sees his friends abandoning him one by one.

21/4/87

A big party is held at Nikki's place. Slash wakes up in Nikki's spare bedroom with lots of girls, and having wet the bed in his sleep.

27/4/87

In his drug-induced paranoid state, Nikki has heavy wooden shutters fitted to all the windows on his house. He thinks about going to rehab but feels he has too much to do. He even injected heroin into a vein in his penis a few nights ago, thinking he looked fantastic. He sleeps with a gun and puts it in his mouth tonight and considers pulling the trigger to end the insanity.

As an intravenous heroin user, Nikki uses the popular hemorrhoid symptom relief gel Preparation H on his tender injection marks to soothe the soreness, as well as under his eyes to keep any inflammation swelling down.

1/5/87

Unable to stop binging on cocaine and heroin, Nikki calls drug recovery specialist Bob Timmons, who comes over to help him. Part of the twelve-stop program for curing addiction is accepting there is a greater power in the world than you, so Bob asks Nikki to get on his knees and pray to God to lose this obsession with drugs – Nikki refuses. Doing $500 or more of heroin a day, he hatches a plan to cut his intake by more and more each day, and go on to methadone when low enough so he can get off completely.

9/5/87

With his grandfather Tom living at his home for a week, Nikki registers for a thirty-day program in Burbank. He plans on only taking methadone for three or four days and then going cold turkey to get off drugs. He throws away all his drug utensils.

11/5/87

The title track of the new Mötley Crüe album Girls, Girls, Girls is released as the first single, backed with another new song called Sumthin' For Nuthin'. Girls, Girls, Girls peaks at number twelve on the U.S. charts, which is the highest placing for a Crüe single to date as it spends fifteen weeks on the charts.

When Mick Mars originally came up with the song, he didn't like it very much, so he went home and demolished a bottle of Jack Daniels before coming up with a new lick. The soloing at the end of the song drops off, as Mick falls off his stool while recording it. The opening motorbike sound was recorded in the courtyard of Conway Studios with Tom Werman revving one of the guys' Harleys. For the outro bike sample, Werman rode Vince's Harley in Franklin Canyon and recorded the bike shifting through its gears.

Vince plays a demo version of the song to his friend Michael Peters, owner of the Pure Platinum chain of strip clubs, and he promises to play the song on the hour, every hour, in every strip club he owns; a promise he is said to have kept to this day.

The subsequent Girls, Girls, Girls video clip is quickly banned by MTV, due to topless strippers dancing, and they opt for a censored version for airplay instead that Mötley has up their sleeve. The video also sees the avid motorcycling Crüe riding their Harley's, having recently formed their own Harley Davidson riding club called the Dark Angels. They even have their stage clothing designer Ray Brown make some studded leather jackets with the words Dark Angels framing band mascot Allister Fiend on the back, based on the Hell's Angels patch design. Vince's new mud-wrestling girlfriend Sharise Ruddell appears in the video, as well as on the inner-sleeve of the new Girls, Girls, Girls album. Professional female wrestler and wet t-shirt queen Quisha also features in the video.

14/5/87

A Girls, Girls, Girls listening party is held inside The Body Shop strip club at 8250 Sunset Boulevard, Hollywood to celebrate the band's fourth album release set for the following day. Sick as a dog, Nikki takes a handful of painkillers and lots of whisky to get him through the event. After dogging the band in his press interviews, Yngwie Malmsteen shows up at the event, so Mötley has security throw him out. The much-anticipated album ships Platinum and debuts at number five; the highest debuting album since Stevie Wonder's Hotter Than July opened at number four in 1980. It's also the highest debut of a metal album since Led Zeppelin's epic The Song Remains The Same debuted at number three in 1976. Girls, Girls, Girls eventually climbs to number two but is unable to dislodge Whitney Houston's second consecutive number one album, titled Whitney. The Crüe hears that retailers were ready to report their album as number one when Clive Davis says he will fly all of the retail heads to Australia first-class and put them up in five-star hotels to see Whitney Houston, if they report her as number one. The band feels that Girls should have been their first number one album.

Girls, Girls, Girls features gospel singers performing backup vocals, as well as street noises recorded in downtown Los Angeles. Ted Nugent's band member Dave Amato also contributes back up vocals, as does Pat Torpey, who previously drummed for Robert Plant and Belinda Carlisle, and later joins Mr. Big. The final track on the album is a live version of Elvis Presley's hit Jailhouse Rock, recorded at Long Beach Arena, California on the previous Theatre of Pain U.S. tour. Nikki comes up with the design for the album cover, which once again displays a new Mötley Crüe logo, this time designed by Chris Polentz, over a photo of the band on their Harley Davidson motorbikes taken by Barry Levine.

15/5/87
Nikki gets a German short-haired pointer puppy and calls it Whisky.

21/5/87

Tommy dreams that he was playing the drums upside-down, and he wants to turn it into reality. He tells management and hopes they can design a drum kit that can spin around like a gyroscope while he's playing it.

Later that night, one of three dogs owned by Tommy's wife Heather is shot twice and killed by someone who apparently waits for her to leave their Woodland Hills home. Police investigate who killed her Maltese toy spaniel.

29/5/87

After rehcarsals, Gene Simmons drives over to Nikki's house in his new black Rolls Royce and they write songs together.

6/87

In preparation for the forthcoming tour, Vince sells his Porter Ranch house and rents an apartment in Hollywood, putting most of his possessions in storage. Mick loses sixteen pounds by halving his alcohol consumption, but he prepares large bottles for the tour labeled Mars Ade; his own cocktail of tequila, orange juice and grenadine. He stores his car at the house of his friend, who smashes the passenger's side and asks for $500 to look after it while he is away. With lawyers and accountants pushing him hard for child support payments, Mick still finds himself broke, even though the band has now sold millions of albums.

5/6/87

Inspired by Merry Clayton's work with the Rolling Stones, and Madeline Bell and Doris Trio's backing vocals in Humble Pie, the Crüe decides to employee a couple of back-up singers for the tour. They work with a female vocalist Bree Howard who previously toured with Jimmy Buffet as a percussionist and has also sung with Robbie Nevil, but they decide against her joining as Nikki starts having sex with her. They audition more than ten singers in their Burbank practice facility to the song Dancin' On Glass, before Donna McDaniel and Emi Canyn are chosen today and dubbed the Nasty Habits. Nikki's concept is to have three sexy women on stage with their top-half dressed in a nun's habit and dressed nastily from the chest down, but the two girls wear a range of skimpy clothes on stage instead. Emi tells them at the audition that she has only been married for six months, but wants to go on tour to get away from her husband. Vince tries his luck with both of the girls at the audition but gets knocked back.

17/6/87

Vittoria Hohman of Florida files a lawsuit against Mötley Crüe and concert promoter Beach Club Promotions after Mötley's performance at St. Petersburg's Bayfront Center on 20 December 1985 caused her to lose all hearing in one ear and partial hearing in the other by the time she left the concert. Her fourteen-year-old daughter Kellie suffered temporary damage as well after they sat front-row for the show, less than three meters from the stage right next to a wall of speakers. The case is settled out of court by mutual agreement two years later and the band's insurance company compensates her with around $30,000.

Rolling Stone magazine holds a photo shoot with the band in Tuscon, Arizona for an upcoming cover story.

After being clean for over a month, Nikki has a little shot of heroin in his hotel bathroom, to celebrate being off heroin.

19/6/87

The Girls, Girls, Girls U.S. tour kicks off in Tucson, Arizona with Whitesnake in support, after a week of technical run-throughs and rehearsals at arenas in San Diego and Arizona. The show is powered by the largest amount of PA ever taken on the road by any band. Theatrics include a giant inflatable Harley Davidson motorbike and a spinning drum cage for Tommy, which was developed in conjunction with former navy submarine hydraulics specialist Chris Deiter, after many stage set design companies told them it couldn't be done. It is built for about $80,000 by welding the cage to a forklift, mounted on yolks from a garbage truck, connected by a heap of cables and pumped into flight with hydraulics fluid. During rehearsals Tommy would get dizzy as he played upside-down in his spinning cage, but he soon overcame this by staring at a spot while spinning; something he recalled from his ballet lessons as a child. The cage can only spin five revolutions forward before spinning back to unwind the microphone cables. Nikki and Tommy scull from Jack Daniels bottles onstage as part of the show, and Jack Daniels even release a promotionally labeled Mötley Crüe bottle as part of their affiliation. Not in great shape, Nikki vomits on the side of stage during Tommy's solo, as his body is not geared to going full tilt yet. His girlfriend Vanity goes back home after embarrassing the band as she dances in the photo pit during their set.

Rather than Mötley traveling between shows on a tour bus, they use an eighteen-seat Gulfstream One jet, sporting a Mötley logo design by artist Tyler with a scantily-dressed cowgirl riding a bomb, a-la World War II bomber planes. Piloted by Tommy Beal for Aces High, it is fitted out with beds, couches and a black leather interior. The stewardess lays out drugs and drinks on each band member's meal tray before they board; white wine and zombie dust (a mix of the sedative Halcyon and cocaine) for Nikki, a cocktail and zombie dust for Tommy, vodka for Mick and a sleeping pill for Vince.

The tour plans to head to Japan in December after the U.S. dates, then on to Europe in January. They then schedule a return to Los Angeles on the 1 February for a couple of months off before a further American leg with Guns N' Roses in support.

22/6/87
Girls, Girls, Girls is released in Australia.

24/6/87
Tommy has sex with Tawny Kitaen, the girlfriend of Whitesnake front man David Coverdale. He knew her from days when she used to do drugs with Ratt's Robbin Crosby.

The road becomes 'the airport blowjob tour' as there's always a line of girls waiting for the band at the airport, so they take them into the bathrooms of the private airports.

Nikki's tech Tim Luzzi goes on stage every night in a priest's robe while Nikki grabs his hair, tilts his head back and pretends to make him drink Jack Daniels.

7/87

Tired of the pain from his degenerative bone disease, chronic depression sets in with Mick. When anti-depressants from psychologists and anaesthetics from pain management counsellors don't assist, he turns towards alcohol more, as his own secret medicine. He sculls six shots of vodka then a can of Coke before he goes on stage every night. He then drinks a glass of straight vodka from the side of the stage during the show, before drinking his Mars Ade once the show is over. Mick also starts seeing Nasty Habit backup singer Emi Canyn, much to the rest of the band's disapproval, since they have a rule to not sleep with anyone who works for the band. They punish the couple by pouring drinks on them and smearing food over their luggage, amongst other things. Mick feels disillusioned and disgusted in his band-mates. He considers walking out of Mötley Crüe.

Vanity tells the press during an interview that she is engaged to Nikki Sixx and they are going to marry on Christmas Eve. He sports the Roman numeral V tattooed on his upper right arm for Vanity, but feels she always makes his life difficult as their relationship is purely based on drugs and entertainment instead of love or even friendship. She has also lost a kidney to her drug habit, and is starting to lose her sight and hearing as well.

16/7/87

After their Chicago concert, the Mötley band members head to a transvestite bar where they drink vodka shots, eat caviar and laugh at all the characters of the night. Two twins make out with each other in front of them as entertainment. Fans hanging outside the club for hours prompt the police to come in. When they see silver trays with silver lids covering lines of cocaine on them, one of the officers says they love the band and if any cops try to bust them while they're in Chicago, just call them.

18/7/87

Video footage for the upcoming single Wild Side is shot during the show at Market Square Arena in Indianapolis, Indiana. Vince informs the crowd they are going to film as cameramen enter the stage. The song is played twice, allowing all the aspects of the show to be captured for the video. Director Wayne Isham has cameras set up to capture all angles of the Crüe's live concert. He wants to put a camera on Nikki's bass but he doesn't let him, so he puts it on Mick's guitar instead. A huge plexiglass ball with a camera in it gets tossed around in the crowd capturing crazy shots before it gets broken. Wild Side is the first Crüe song to be recorded using computer technology, as Tommy played a chunky guitar riff and chopped it into sixteenth notes.

22/7/87

Mötley's debut album Too Fast For Love reaches Platinum status, the last of their four albums to break the million-copies-sold barrier.

23/7/87

John Corabi's wife Valerie gives birth to their son, who they name Ian Karac Corabi.

26/7/87

Mötley plays a great outdoor show at Buckeye Lake in Ohio in front of forty thousand people with Whitesnake and Anthrax in support.

28/7/87

Arriving home for a few day's break, Nikki writes a song called

A is For Asshole, and can feel depression building inside him as an accumulation of issues.

5/8/87
Returning to their hotel in Philadelphia after their concert, Tommy and Nikki lock all the doors of their limo as their driver gets out to open their doors. They then drive off around the parking lot with the driver chasing them, before crashing it into the hotel gate.

10/8/87
Wild Side is released as a single with Five Years Dead as the B-side track. The song was written at SIR Rehearsal Studios.

13/8/87
Paul Stanley from Kiss joins the Crüe on stage at Meadowlands Arena in New Jersey to sing Jailhouse Rock with Vince.

15/8/87
In his Parker Meridian hotel room in New York after the Mötley show in Rhode Island, Nikki shoots up too much heroin and overdoses. Vanity finds him passed out in the bathroom with a needle lying next to him.

20/8/87
Mötley brings out Robbin Crosby from Ratt to play guitar on Jailhouse Rock with them at Madison Square Garden in New York City.

25/8/87
Before the Crüe's show in Rochester, New York, someone breaks into Vince's dressing room and steals his clothes and wallet with five thousand dollars in it. When he then goes to get some dinner, Vince slams a glass jar of Grey Poupon dijon mustard against the backstage wall, when he sees there's no French's yellow mustard for the sandwich he is making, even though he'd been asking for the rider to be changed for weeks.

The smash severs many tendons, nerves and an artery, almost cutting one finger off Vince's right hand. The show is cancelled and he is airlifted to the Hand Centre in Baltimore, where he undergoes an eight-hour operation the next day. Management tells press that a bottle of mustard exploded in his hand while he made himself a hamburger. Vince wears a full cast up to his elbow for a month, and bandages for three months following his specialist surgery.

Aerosmith releases their ninth studio album Permanent Vacation that includes a track called Dude (Looks Like A Lady), which was written about Vince Neil. At the Palladium nightclub on E 14th Street in New York City one night, Aerosmith frontman Steven Tyler once saw Vince from a distance and thought he was a woman, until he noticed a lot of girls coming on to him. Intrigued at how he picked up chicks while looking like one, the two met and chatted. The Crüe's repeated use of the Californian word 'dude' was noted and taken as inspiration for the hit song. Steve Tyler and Joe Perry leave a note on the windshield of the Crüe's tour plane one night, telling them that they are crashing and burning and they can help them since they have been there before. The Crüe laughs-off the warning from their idols.

26/8/87

Nikki tells Vanity on the phone that it is over between them, but they still see each other from time to time and do drugs.

9/87

Mötley Crüe is hit with a $5,000 lawsuit by a woman claiming to have suffered "severe hearing dysfunction and mental anguish" after attending a Mötley Crüe concert with her daughter.

16/9/87

The Crüe's Girls, Girls, Girls album is certified Double-Platinum, having now sold more than two million copies in the USA.

Karen Dumont stays at Nikki's house to keep an eye on things while he is on tour.

1/10/87
Shortly before 8am, an earthquake tremor measuring 5.9 on the Richter scale occurs twelve miles east from downtown Los Angeles, directly under the city of Whittier, causing eight deaths, $350 million in property damage, and leaving 2,200 people homeless. At home between shows on the tour, Nikki runs out of his house naked, grabbing only his most important possession: his freebase pipe. He has to break a window on his side door to get back inside his house after locking his keys in.

6/10/87
Nikki rides his Harley to the band's sold-out hometown show at the Grand Western Forum. As he arrives at the venue, a cop pulls him over and says he was speeding. When Nikki can't produce a driver's license, the cop says he's going to jail; Nikki says if he's not on stage in an hour there'll be a riot. He arrests Nikki and puts him in the back of a police car, before Doc McGhee sorts the situation and has Nikki apologise to the cop for swearing at him.

10/10/87
Having not slept in days from drugs, Nikki skips his flight on the Mötley plane as the band travels to play a huge, prestigious show at Oakland Stadium. Out of his mind on cocaine, he feels as though he's going to have a heart attack. Doc organises a later flight on a commercial jet and when Nikki finally arrives at the stadium in a mess, they hold a band meeting and confront him about his excessive drug use. Tour security chief Fred Saunders later says, "There were countless management meetings called during the Girls tour just to try to work out what to do with Nikki. By the end of the tour, I was hiring security guards at each hotel and just leaving two of them on his door permanently."

15/10/87

Mötley's show at the Tacoma Dome in Washington State is filmed and in later years becomes one of their most widely bootlegged concert videos. A fan dies from a drug overdose at the venue on the night. Nikki's mum attends the show, after visiting him at his hotel with his sister Ceci and her two young boys: two-year-old Jake and baby Caleb. In a drugged-out state, Nikki tells them to go away and calls them every name under the sun.

17/10/87

On a day off between shows in Canada, Nikki and Tommy shoot up a lot of cocaine and heroin. When they run out, they shoot up Jack Daniels.

19/10/87

You're All I Need is released as the third single from Girls, Girls, Girls and is the first time Mötley have so many singles released from an album. The song peaks at number eighty three during its eight-week stay on the U.S. charts. The video for the song features young, longhaired actor Geno Andrews playing a jealous lover who gets arrested for killing his girl. (A couple of years later he features as a dishwasher in Poison's video for Nothin' But A Good Time.)

All In The Name Of... is used as the B-side on the single, which is said to have been written about the young porn star Tracii Lords. It is also the Crüe's opening song of their set list being performed live on the tour.

21/10/87

At 6am in Winnipeg, Mötley participates in a live segment for Japanese TV. The band is interviewed by video-jockey Mako Hattori in the freezing cold outside a strip club on Provencher Boulevard in St. Boniface and beamed back live to 30 million Japanese viewers. The band then runs inside the club and performs in synch to Wild Side with four strippers grinding.

After their show in Winnipeg, Tommy goes to Nikki's hotel room with Fred Saunders where they sit around drinking and snorting. After a while, Nikki sneaks out of his room and douses another room's door with lighter fluid and hair spray, before lighting it, knocking and running off thinking it was Rich Fisher's door. It sets off the fire alarms and scares a young Chinese guy and his son who open the door that is ablaze. Nikki ducks back into his room and laughs at all the commotion.

25/10/87
Tommy and Nikki do a radio interview with Joey Vendetta on Toronto radio station Q107 to promote their upcoming concert. They then head to a club called Rock'n'Roll Heaven, where a fist fight develops after a patron makes a disparaging remark to Tommy about his wife Heather. Club management kicks everyone out except Mötley and their crew, who keep drinking until 4am.

27/10/87
David Coverdale from support band Whitesnake joins Mötley on stage in Montreal for their rendition of Jailhouse Rock, as Whitesnake plays their final show in support and Guns N' Roses get set to take over. Whitesnake was originally only going to play a few early dates on the tour, but Mötley management happily increased their fee from $4,000 per night to $10,000 so they would stay on the tour, as much as they bored the Crüe members.

29/10/87
Steve Deske and Mary Ann Rizzo win MTV's Mötley Cruise to Nowhere competition and join the Crüe on a five-hour luxury boat cruise in the Bermuda Triangle, following a private cocktail party at the ritzy Elbow Beach Hotel the night before. Two wild cross-dressers attend the party, one who designed costumes for the band and happened to win a contest and one who later goes on to front The Toilet Boys as Miss Guy. The contest winners

are driven around in limousines and given $1,000 spending money.

After the cruise, Vince and Sharise spend the weekend on Florida's Captiva Island before the Girls, Girls, Girls tour resumes.

31/10/87

Mötley Crüe shoots a video with Wayne Isham for You're All I Need on Halloween. The video clip is based on the movie Taxi Driver and is further inspired by the self-destructive relationship of Sid Vicious and Nancy Spungeon. After viewing the first version of the video that doesn't feature the band at all, the record company instructs them to add some band footage, which is shot at Wayne Isham's studio. When finally released, the video is banned by MTV due to its graphical content, particularly of one scene showing a body bag being zipped up, coupled with the nature of the song's lyrics.

3/11/87

In Mobile, Alabama, Guns N' Roses plays their first show supporting Mötley Crüe.

Skid Row approaches John Corabi this month to join them as their front-man but end up recruiting Sebastian Bach from the band Kid Wikkid instead, who recently supported Mötley Crüe in Canada.

7/11/87

After their show at Lakefront Arena, Nikki and Slash go into the French Quarter of New Orleans. They get wasted in some bars, after getting refused entry at the Dungeon because Nikki cut the bra off the owner's girlfriend last time he was there.

9/11/87

Nikki and Slash drink shots in their hotel's bar for hours on their night off, when they start wrestling. Nikki falls on top of Slash and when he wakes up next morning in Tommy's drum tech Spider's bed, he feels pain in his neck. Doctors tell Slash he has four dislocated vertebrae.

19/11/87
After throwing up spaghetti on the bar at the Ritz Carlton hotel in Atlanta, Slash immediately orders another shot to keep drinking with Nikki.

20/11/87
Tommy and Nikki cut Doc McGhee's hotel bed in half with a knife, so when he gets into it later that night it collapses. Nikki tries to throw Fred's bed out the window and gets a black eye for his trouble, while Mick tries to jump out his hotel window. Wondering why he has no pubic hair, Doc tells Nikki the next day that they all had their penises out on the bar and poured Jack Daniels on them and lit them on fire.

28/11/87
On the Mötley jet traveling from Fort Myers to Fort Lauderdale after their show, Nikki taunts Nasty Habit Emi and her religious ways by standing in the middle of the jet with his pants down and begging God to strike him down. As Emi cries, Tommy gets the pilot to do a barrel roll.

29/11/87
To celebrate the final Guns N' Roses support show, the Crüe surprises them by having about twenty-five pyro blasts kick in as they commence Welcome to the Jungle. Lead singer Axl Rose wears a Mötley Crüe t-shirt on stage. After the Florida show, they party in a conference room with a heap of booze and about two ounces of cocaine that they snort off the backs of six or seven naked girls before making out with them. They trash the room as they leave and Tommy takes some pills and passes out, so Rich Fisher pushes him in a wheel chair through the airport and onto the plane at noon the next day to head back home.

10/12/87

Mötley lands in Japan to commence their Girls, Girls, Girls tour with some press commitments. Tommy is busted with some marijuana in his drum kit and is bailed out of the situation by their Japanese tour promoter Mr. Udo without any charges being laid. When they get to the hotel, Tommy drops a wine bottle out of a tenth storey window. Nikki feels sick, sweats a lot, and cramps up with pain because he has no heroin.

11/12/87

Whilst still on probation, Vince downs a pitcher of Kamikaze cocktail at a Roppongi restaurant, before flipping a table over on four Yakuza mafia gangsters in suits after he thought they were talking about him. They subsequently pull guns from their waists and aim them at Vince from on top of the over-turned table. Mötley's security chief Fred Saunders rolls Vince onto the floor and out into their waiting limo. Vince later wakes up naked on the floor of his hotel room, not knowing what had happened. Next morning, he discovers he is missing his $12,000 diamond and gold Rolex watch that management gave him after lasting three months without a drink following his tragic car accident three years earlier. He also sees the girlfriend of the Yakuza that he took back to the hotel has gone.

Later in the night, Nikki gets arrested on his birthday in Tokyo, after being involved in a couple of fist fights at The Lexington Queen club in the Roppongi district. The first is with Tommy, who believes Nikki hit him in the mouth, while Nikki feels Tommy was so drunk that he fell over before he ever connected. The second is with an American tourist, as he smashes him in the nose before his head hits a steel pole, cracking it open and spilling blood over his eyes. Mick leaves the club wearing the owner's Godzilla mask and terrorises people in the street with his pants around his ankles, urinating along the side of the road. He stomps on glasses and tries to breathe fire from his rear.

14/12/87

Heading back to Tokyo by train after their Osaka show, Tommy and Nikki down fifteen or so bottles of sake before they pour Jack Daniels over the heads of unsuspecting commuters, including back-up singer Emi. They order curry and smear it all over the walls in the high-speed Bullet Train, amongst other riotous behaviour. Nikki shouts angrily at Mick and suddenly throws a Jack Daniels bottle at Mr. Udo, after he tells them to settle down, but it misses its mark by a long shot and smashes into a businessman commuter, who collapses to the ground screaming with blood streaming from a wound in the back of the his head. Mr. Udo calms the Terror Twins, Nikki and Tommy, by pressing his thumb into the back of their necks. When the train stops in Tokyo, lots of Japanese Riot Squad police run along side their carriage, along with many fans. They handcuff Nikki and after Doc McGhee tells them he is his manager, they cuff him also, placing them both in a police car. Tommy hassles the police so he can go with Nikki too–to no avail. In jail, Nikki asks Doc how he likes his tattoos and asks if he should show the police.

15/12/87

Mr. Udo comes to the police station at 4am and they sign an apology note for the businessman who was hit with the bottle. When Doc and Nikki are before the sergeant with a translator that Mr. Udo brought with him, they tell the police that the bottle accidentally slipped out of Nikki's hand and broke. He says he will also tell the American press how hospitable the Japanese people are on his return to the USA; instead of translating Nikki's question to the sergeant of "If my balls were on your chin, where do you think my dick would be?" Nikki and Doc are released from jail at 5am but Doc has to take care of paperwork taking him until night. Just before he crashes in bed back at his hotel, a drunken Vince bangs on his door telling him that he should fire the travel agent because he was trying to make out with the Yakuza's girlfriend, but his girlfriend Sharise was in his room, having just arrived from the U.S. without his knowledge. Doc punches Vince in the face and closes the door.

16/12/87
Nikki calls the hotel front desk and complains about the fans banging on his window; however his room is on the twenty-sixth floor.

19/12/87
After winding up their Japanese tour the previous night by playing the last of three nights at the famous Budokan in Tokyo, Tommy heads back to Los Angeles to spend Christmas with Heather in their lavish home in a Woodland Hills gated community. The two-storey Tudor style house was newly built for them last year. Decorated in a Victorian Country style, it has five bedrooms and five baths covering just under five-thousand-square-feet. Tommy has a twenty-three-foot-long recording studio in the attic, plus a cabinet full of sound equipment with speakers fitted in the rocks by the swimming pool and three waterfalls.

Mick and Emi Canyn look forward to spending some quality time at home off the road and away from the hassles of other band members, while Vince looks forward to spending time with girlfriend Sharise; the mud wrestler from the Tropicana.

With no lady nor home life to go back to, Nikki decides he is going on a solo tour of Asia to enjoy drugs and prostitutes with nothing but a packet of condoms, commencing in Hong Kong, followed by Malaysia, Beijing China, then a finale in Bangkok. Doc McGhee tries to stop Nikki from going but Mr. Udo says he will accompany Nikki on the journey. Doc then draws the short straw with Doug Thaler after feeling obliged that one of them needs to join them as well. Mr. Udo sits next to Nikki on the way to Hong Kong and tells him that the last time he saw a friend in the same state as Nikki, he died. Nikki shrugs it off but becomes more interested as he learns it was former James Gang and Deep Purple guitarist Tommy Bolin, who overdosed in 1976 at twenty five years of age. Once they arrive, they go to a Chinese restaurant that Mr. Udo says is one of the best in the world.

20/12/87

Nikki goes shopping for antiques and buys a Chinese table made from cherry wood with pearl cherry blossom inlays for his dining room. He later meets Doc and Mr. Udo for a few drinks in the hotel bar before they go to a whorehouse that poses as a strip club. He hears a band playing a Mötley Crüe song as they are shown into a private room with four bottles of Cristal champagne, two bottles of Jack Daniels, a bottle of vodka and huge plates of food. They order different fetish-styled prostitutes to entertain them, like one would order food. Nikki scores a gram of cocaine and a quarter of 'china white' heroin from the girls, once Doc and Mr. Udo have left. He then orders ten prostitutes in Nazi helmets for Doc that arrive at his hotel room while he is on the phone to his wife, and more for Mr. Udo. Nikki later returns to the hotel with some of the prostitutes and passes out.

21/12/87

After waking up, throwing up and shooting up the last of his cocaine stash, Nikki discovers the prostitutes stole his cash, before he meets Doc and Mr. Udo in the hotel lobby where they tell him of their disgust in the prostitutes he ordered for them the previous night. Mr. Udo flies back to Tokyo while Doc organises flights back to the U.S. the following day, thus ending the Sixx solo party tour. At night, Nikki wanders the Hong Kong streets with his female translator Li, intent on looking for drugs, when he comes across a soothsayer dressed in a brown robe at the end of a long alley off Wanchai Road. He pays four Hong Kong dollars and the old soothsayer runs his hand across Nikki's before curling it up and pushing it away. He says to the translator that Nikki will die before the end of the year and he can't change his ways. Nikki asks Li if those guys are just to lure tourists in Hong Kong but she sadly tells him they are never wrong. They head back to the hotel and Nikki calls his dealer in Los Angeles to instruct him to meet him tomorrow with the usual $10,000 worth of heroin and some cocaine (along with syringes) when he lands back in the United States.

22/12/87

Nikki flies into Los Angeles International Airport from Tokyo, where he gets high on a 10cc shot in the limo that picks him up to take him to his recently purchased house, which former girlfriend Nicole chose eighteen months ago. He looks in his mirror and sees himself disintegrating; his hair falling out in clumps, needle tracks down his arms, and a puffy alcoholic face.

Wanting to escape his loneliness with a night on the town, he calls friends Robbin Crosby from Ratt and Slash from Guns N' Roses. Nikki's silver limousine picks up Robbin from his home and they head to the Franklin Plaza Hotel where the homeless Guns N' Roses stay. He greets Slash at the room's door (the one next to Dave Ellefson from Megadeth's room) with a bottle of whiskey and an antique beaver-hair top hat that he had thrown up on in the limo on the way. They drive to the Cathouse club with Slash's Scottish girlfriend Sally McLaughlan, scoring some heroin that they pick up from Robbin's dealer on the way. While at the club for hours, the guys often go in and out to the limo to do drugs. The last time they do it, they don't come back for Sally, so she walks back to Franklin Plaza on her own on her first night in Los Angeles.

The guys head back to the hotel with some fans following them from the club. Robbin's dealer meets them there with some Persian heroin he just got. Sally arrives back at the hotel and furiously tries to talk with Slash who is passed out on the couch, so Nikki goes into Steven Adler's suite with the dealer. The dealer ties Nikki off and shoots him up, turning him blue in an instant. Nikki knocks on Slash's door and collapses on the floor when Sally opens it. With one look at Nikki turned blue, the dealer jumps out of the hotel room window and over the balcony, running down the street yelling out that he just killed Nikki Sixx.

With Slash paralytic, Steve Adler and Sally start beating on his chest to revive him and Adler slaps him in the face with the cast on his broken arm. They drag him into the bathroom and Adler runs off, so Sally tries to get Nikki into the shower to get cold water onto him. Slash comes into the bathroom, sees Nikki and starts freaking out as he lost a friend Todd to a heroin overdose a few months ago. Sally gives Nikki mouth-to-mouth resuscitation over the bath while trying to calm Slash, who smashes the shower screen, sending shattered glass all over Sally and Nikki. After punching Slash out, Sally yells for someone to call 911 as a last effort to save his life from an overdose. The paramedics arrive quickly and take over from Sally's mouth-to-mouth, ripping his t-shirt off to give him adrenaline as they take him out of the room. The police then question everyone in Axl's room, not spotting a bag of dope and a vial of cocaine.

After being dead for some minutes, at the hotel named the same as his birth name–Franklin, Nikki has an out-of-body experience. He hears, "We're losing him" and tries to sit up to see what is going on, before shooting upright and slowly ascending towards bright light all above him. He sees his body on the gurney covered head-to-toe and being pushed into the ambulance by the paramedics who had to pronounce him dead. He also sees the fans that had followed them, as well as his silver limo.

Nikki's limo driver Boris calls Vince telling him what the dealer said and that he saw Nikki being wheeled out into the ambulance with a sheet over his face. News of Nikki's death spreads fast, quickly reaching radio stations, which announce Nikki's death. Not long after that, Mötley tour manager Rich Fisher calls Vince and tells him of the overdose. Tears roll down Vince's face. Slash calls Tommy and tells him that they tried to do everything to keep him alive but the paramedics wheeled him out with a sheet over his face. Doug Thaler calls his co-manager Doc McGhee, who has just finished dinner with Bob Krasnow of Elektra Records, and tells him of the death.

Rich Fisher calls a hung-over Mick Mars and breaks the news to him that Nikki is dead, asking him to call England and cancel the band's forthcoming European tour for him, which is due to commence on January 10. Mick calls Kerrang! magazine and makes up some lame excuses for why they aren't coming over any more.

After almost giving him up for dead, a second attempt of a double-dose jab of adrenalin brings his out-of-body vision down fast through the roof of the ambulance with a painful jerk, as the shots kick-start his life again. He opens his eyes to see a needle in each side of his chest and hears a man say that no one will die in his ambulance, before he passes out.

When he awakes in Cedar-Sinai Hospital to a policeman shining a torch in his eyes and asking where he got the drugs, he abuses him and is told he's not being held on any charges. Against medical advice, Nikki pulls the tubes from his nose and the I.V. out of his arm, before signing himself out of hospital wearing only his leather pants.

Outside in the hospital car park, he sees two teenage fans crying on the kerbside and holding candles because they heard on the radio that he had died. Speechless that Nikki is alive, the girls drive him home to Van Nuys in their Mazda and lend him one of their jackets. They hear his death being reported on radio stations on the way, while Nikki realises that he does have millions of people that do care about him. He gets dropped home at 5:45am, much to the amazement of Karen Dumont, who received the bad news call from Doug Thaler a couple of hours earlier. Apologising that he couldn't find his key, Nikki goes straight to his answering machine and changes the message to say, "Hey, it's Nikki. I'm not home because I'm dead" before shooting up from a lump of heroin stored in his medical cabinet. He passes out again.

The band's accountant Chuck Shapiro calls Vince saying a reporter called him for an obituary quote. Chuck puts Vince on hold while he calls the hospital to verify, returning to tell him the nurse just saw him leave.

23/12/87

Doc McGhee finds out Nikki has escaped from hospital so he heads to his office and calls in Doug Thaler. They cancel Mötley's European tour, blaming exhaustion as the official reason. Nikki wakes up on his blood-covered bathroom floor with his heroin needle still dangling out of his bloodied arm. He hears his answering machine play its message to Doc, who had arrived at his house with Doug, finding him passed out again in the bathroom while Karen had gone to work. They talk him into coming to Doc's house in Tarzana for detox. Bob Timmons works with him at Doc's house while Steven Tyler from Aerosmith calls daily, telling him he is going to die forever, as an effort to bully him into cleaning up.

24/12/87

Tommy and Heather have a big disagreement on Christmas Eve. Tommy realises he needs to become sober in order to save his marriage, as he is at the point where he has become violent when under the influence of alcohol.

Doc soon calls a band meeting in his living room and management presents a united front, telling them they will be paying back the European concert promoters for the cancelled shows, out of their own pockets, then advising they will quit if the band doesn't straighten up. Every band member agrees to go to rehab, and they make a pact that they all have to be sober before recording of the next album commences.

25/12/87

Nikki spends Christmas at his Sherman Oaks home with Karen Dumont, Sally McLaughlan and Slash.

1988

1/88

Tommy Lee is the first band member to check into rehab as he enters a facility in Tucson called Cottonwood. On his second day, a doctor brings the demons of his addiction to the surface and Tommy breaks down when he realises how powerful the force of his addiction is, which has been controlling him for years. When he sees a sign saying Silence = Death, he thinks back to his childhood and being punished by being sent to his room and not spoken to.

After a week, the other band members fly to Cottonwood to be together, at the suggestion of Bob Timmons, and they are soon standing in a circle with their arms around each other singing The Rolling Stones song You Can't Always Get What You Want as part of their therapy. After the song, Nikki Sixx's resentment towards his parents kept bottled inside causes him to break down when the counsellor asks them to visualise themselves as little boys.

Pennsylvanian resident Matthew John Trippe claims Crüe managers Doc McGhee and Doug Thaler decided to bring him in as a new Nikki after he was unable to continue after his serious car crash in mid-1983. He files a lawsuit against McGhee Enterprises, Inc. citing civil theft and other relief, claiming royalties that were never paid for songs he claims he wrote. These include Danger, Knock 'Em Dead Kid, Girls Girls Girls, You're All I Need, Dancing On Glass, and Wild Side. Trippe has a criminal history of drugs and has been in and out of mental institutions for some time.

Doc McGhee is arrested on a charge of assisting to smuggle twenty nine thousand pounds of marijuana into North Carolina from Colombia on July 7, 1982 via a shrimp boat, prior to his association with the Crüe. He has previously been busted for bringing a shipment of cocaine into the state of Louisiana, so this is his second drug trafficking charge. After pleading guilty,

McGhee receives a five-year suspended prison sentence, a fine of $15,000, and is ordered to set up an anti-drugs foundation. McGhee calls it the Make A Difference Foundation.

Vince Neil finally completes his two hundred hours of community service and probation period, stemming from his vehicular manslaughter charge after his December 1984 car crash.

21/1/88
Vince joins Guns N' Roses on stage at The Cathouse in Hollywood to sing the night's final song - the AC/DC classic Whole Lotta Rosie. The concert is the first for drummer Steven Adler since breaking his arm.

17/2/88
A twelve-year-old fan from Hollywood, Florida sets his legs on fire while trying to imitate the shot in Mötley's Live Wire video clip, where Nikki plays guitar with his high heeled leather boots alight. The boy suffers burns over ten percent of his body. Mötley Crüe issues a statement saying the band's stunts should not be tried at home.

2/88
Although Mick Mars goes along with the group meetings and therapy in the early stages, he finds his own form of quitting works better and is a lot cheaper than rehab. He loses twenty pounds and many wrinkles in the first few weeks just by being strong minded and not wanting to drink any more, after becoming so disgusted by the way he looked, how close Nikki came to dying, and the general state of the band.

3/88
Nikki, Tommy and Vince continually check into and out of expensive rehab facilities as they try and stay away from drugs and alcohol. Nikki sells his house on Valley Vista Blvd, Sherman Oaks for $500,000 and moves into a new place in

Hidden Hills, where he writes lots of songs, feels disconnected from reality, and doesn't go out for months at a time.

30/4/88

In a badly hungover state, Vince marries his twenty-three-year-old girlfriend Sharise Lee Ann Ruddell at the Hotel Bel-Air in Los Angeles, by a lake with white swans. Wedding garments are made by Mötley's clothing designer Ray Brown. Sharise grew up in Huntington Beach, California and loved everything about the surf culture, always wearing her bikinis. She met Vince through the Tropicana strip club, where she began working as a round girl holding up signs between bouts, before becoming a mud wrestler there - she was never a stripper. Their first date was a dinner at L'Orangerie then the Comedy Club. Vince reportedly offers to give Sharise $3,000 per month to quit mud wrestling. Pictures of her posing in the pool with Bret Michaels can be seen on the inside sleeve of Poison's Open Up and Say… Ahhh! album. Meanwhile Nikki's former fiancée Vanity graces the cover of this month's issue of Playboy magazine.

Vince and Sharise live in a huge house within the Bell Canyon gated community, near Chatsworth, California. Situated on a five-acre block just forty minutes drive from Los Angeles, the house has a church steeple, its own moat, waterfalls, a stream running through the backyard, a nine-hundred-year-old front door, and a train track that runs big electric trains around the ceilings insides. The problem is that it is haunted, with weird activity taking place particularly in the bedrooms. They get out of there and buy a better place on S Summit Ridge Circle in Chatsworth that overlooks San Fernando Valley. Vince has a car stacking lift system in his three-car garage so he can house six of the thirty-five exotic cars in his collection there.

5/88

Almost three years after Mötley's 1985 concert in Huntsville, Alabama, a $1.3 million lawsuit on behalf of Robby Miller and another young fan injured at the show is lodged at the Limestone County Courthouse in Athens, naming Mötley Crüe, the City of Huntsville, Von Braun Civic Center and concert promoter Sound Seventy Productions as defendants. Nikki testifies and represents the band at the seven-day trial, working with lawyer Patrick Lamar from Lanier Ford Shaver and Payne, who is retained by the band's insurer. Now 17, Miller was a big fan of the group sitting in the audience when he got hit in the face by an object believed to have come from the stage, causing him to lose an eye and have his lip disfigured. Defense attorneys have a table-top sized model of the Theatre of Pain tour stage built by a company in California to use during the trial but the model is heavily damaged during shipment and is glued back together by their lawyer. After a five-male, seven-female jury is unable to reach a decision based on evidence presented, a mistrial is declared. Mötley Crüe reaches an out-of-court financial settlement for an amount that has never been made public.

21/5/88
Vince is one of many hard rock stars who participate in the Rock 'n' Roller Charity Softball game.

7/88
Vince and Sharise are rumoured to be separated, after being married for only three months. The couple find themselves constantly fighting after Sharise gives up her dancing and wrestling work at the Tropicana.

late 88
Vince and Tommy were said to have teamed up with Axl Rose and Slash from Guns N' Roses to collaborate with a band Black & White on their rap song called Rainbow Bar and Girls that was released by Atlantic Records on both cassette-single and 12" maxi single formats. It is actually the band London though, and Lizzie Grey, who co-wrote Public Enemy #1 on Mötley's first album, receives a song writing credit for the track that goes Gold, selling over half a million copies in the U.S. alone, before Atlantic pulls it from sale.

9/88

Finally off heroin, Nikki finds his sobriety to be a terrifying reality. He sees a psychiatrist after becoming very confused and agoraphobic. All his rehab and therapy makes him feel like he's not Nikki Sixx anymore. His therapist suggests he tries a new experimental drug called Prozac to correct his clinical depression and a chemical imbalance in his body, which helps him to start socialising again. He goes on a date with actress Lisa Hartman but it doesn't work out. Nikki invites Eric Stacy from the band Faster Pussycat to move in with him, as he has also been through rehab recently.

10/88

Mötley records a song called Powerful Stuff for the soundtrack of the new Tom Cruise film Cocktail. Production with Tom Werman isn't working out, so they scrap the song, which is then picked up and re-worked by The Fabulous Thunderbirds. The song is included on the soundtrack, and is then released by The Fabulous Thunderbirds a year later and reaches number sixty five on the charts. It features the lead-guitar work of Stevie Ray Vaughan's brother Jimmie.

Now sporting red locks and a large new tattoo of a leopard down his right arm, Tommy features in Sam Kinison's singing debut remake of The Troggs classic, Wild Thing, from his Warner Bros. album Have You Seen Me Lately? The video also features Jon Bon Jovi and Ritchie Sambora of Bon Jovi, Poison's C.C. DeVille, Billy Idol, Rudy Sarzo of Whitesnake, Steven Tyler and Joe Perry of Aerosmith, Slash and Steve Adler from Guns N' Roses, various members of Ratt, and a special appearance by fellow comedian Rodney Dangerfield. It also stars Jessica Hahn, a former girlfriend of Playboy guru Hugh Hefner, as the Wild Thing. Heather forbids Tommy from being anywhere near her after the shoot, due to the shameless way she goes after Tommy on the video set, knowing full well who he is and who he is married to.

8/10/88

Nikki picks up Slash and heads to Imperial Gardens for dinner before they go to Duff's place. They then go to a club called Flaming Colossus and Scream club, before Slash crashes at Nikki's. They head to a shooting range the next day with Nikki's Baretta .380 and a .357.

22/10/88

Nikki visits Mick's house and they write songs including one called Mötley Christmas and a Happy Crüe Year for a hopeful Xmas single. A Rod Stewart-ish type song called Don't Go Away Mad (Just Go Away) and an upbeat strutter called Rattlesnake Shake are also written. They start working on another but get tired, opting to play the blues instead.

11/88

The band and management are unhappy with the working relationship with Tom Werman and feel they now need some fresh blood to get the best out of the band. Quincy Jones is approached but he's busy working on his own project and the next Michael Jackson album. They then meet up with producer Bob Rock, whose influences, thoughts and style are more aligned with the Crüe's. They like his previous work with The Cult, Ted Nugent and particularly Kingdom Come, and decide to work with him on the next Mötley Crüe album, which is to be recorded in his Little Mountain Studios in Vancouver, Canada. It turns out he had always wanted to work on a Mötley record.

12/88

Vince buys Tommy an AK-47 gun for Christmas. All of Mötley, except Mick, boasts large firearms collections, including Berretta semi-automatics, magnums, 12-gauge shotguns, pistols, assault rifles and Uzi's. As a child, Nikki used to hunt with his grandfather using a 30.06 that he made for him.

The Mötley Crüe fan club Safety In Numbers (S.I.N.) ceases its operations.

1989

early 89

Tommy Lee and Nikki Sixx decide to form a music production company called The Terror Twins. They are subsequently bombarded with demo tapes from aspiring bands. Now sober and clear headed, Nikki also starts to listen to a broader range of music that opens his mind to different melodies, runs and hooks. It spawns many new creative ideas.

Mick Mars and Emi Canyn move into a new Californian house together. Dubbed Mars Mountain, the $1.4M home at 14959 Yerba Buena Rd, Malibu sits on top of a 2,000-feet mountain peak providing panoramic views of Lake Sherwood and the surrounding Santa Monica Mountains. The 4-bedroom and 4-bathroom main house, along with a separate 1-bedroom guesthouse, is part of a gated Malibu estate.

27/1/89

Vince Neil sings at the Party Ninja's Benefit Concert in Los Angeles.

2/89

Cathouse club owner Rikki Rachtman sets Nikki up on a blind date with the October 1987 Playboy Playmate Brandi Brandt, after she breaks off with his Cathouse co-owner and Faster Pussycat vocalist Taime Downe when finding a used condom in his garbage. The first night they sleep together, her mum calls. Nikki recognises her Mum's voice, realising it's Bree Howard's daughter he is with, who he had a fling with before the Girls, Girls, Girls tour as they auditioned the Nasty Habits backup singers. He spends more time with her though, feeling emotions he hasn't felt for so long now that he is sober. A couple of weeks later, Nikki moves away from her to begin work on the next Mötley Crüe album.

3/89

The Crüe receives much help from alcohol and drug
rehabilitation specialist Bob Timmons, who became a heroin
addict before he was even a teen, which soon led to him living
on the streets of downtown Los Angeles's Skid Row and
serving time in prison for armed robbery, before he turned his
life around. The band moves to Vancouver, Canada to record
their new album at Little Mountain Studios with Bob Rock
producing. The album is scheduled for a 4th July release. Vince
arrives a day later after Fred Coury from Cinderella invites him
to stay in Hawaii for their Honolulu concert, where he jams
with them on The Rolling Stones classic Jumping Jack Flash.
Vince recently gave Fred a black 1983 Porsche 911 turbo.

One of the first people Nikki sees in Vancouver is actress
Demi Moore, who is shooting the film We're No Angels, and
was the first person to tell him about Alcoholics Anonymous
five years ago. They have dinner with Bob Rock at his home
and he later turns down a ride back to her hotel as he has
Brandi on his mind instead.

A song about Nikki's near-death overdose called Kickstart
My Heart is worked on as the first song for the new album.
Nikki brings it in thinking it doesn't have a hope in hell of
making the album, but it reminds Tommy of Ballroom Blitz by
the Sweet. Bob Rock is meticulous in his work, often making
Mick spend two weeks just doubling a guitar part until he feels
it is perfect, which frustrates Mick. Vince often only gets one
word of a song on tape after a whole day's work due to the
critical and demanding nature of Bob Rock's work ethic that
pushes Mötley to the limit of their abilities for the very first
time.

Also under the guidance of rehab specialist Bob Timmons,
Aerosmith works on their Pump album next door to Mötley, so
they often drink water together and go for jogs after a day in the
studio. The Crüe has a personal weight trainer with them in
Vancouver, over-seeing daily work-outs and runs.

Twenty four songs are demoed, including a two-minute
metal rap song Monstrous rumoured firstly to be on the

Ghostbusters II soundtrack and then also to be the title of the new album. The chorus is inspired by The Wizard of Oz and gets stuck in Nikki's head for weeks. Another rumoured album title is Sex, Sex, and Rock 'n' Roll. They write and record a ten-minute song called Say Yeah about Nikki Sixx impostor Matthew Trippe. A Mick Mars concerto with cello, viola, flute, guitar and drums is also touted for inclusion on the album. Other titles of songs written include Stop Pulling My Chain, Brotherhood, Too Hot to Handle, Rodeo and the bluesy Get It For Free, which is about a girl supposedly selling Bibles door-to-door, except she's selling herself instead.

Nikki phones the guys from Skid Row and asks what they are doing. When they say they are just watching reruns of the TV show Leave It To Beaver, Nikki invites them to come to the studio and sing on the album. They also jam with Cheap Trick at their local show, and invite them to participate on the album.

11/5/89
A thirty-thousand-strong crowd at Vancouver's BC Place stadium goes wild when Vince and Nikki join Skid Row on stage for their encore song Live Wire. Aerosmith's Steve Tyler and Joe Perry join headlining act Bon Jovi for their second encore later in the evening.

19/5/89
Vince tees off with Willie Nelson at the Calabasas Golf and Country Club in California for the Celebrity Invitation Classic golf tournament, as part of the TJ Martell Foundation's Rock 'n' Charity Weekend.

20/5/89
Vince captains the Rockers softball team as they play against Sam Kinison's Rollers in the TJ Martell Foundation's Rock 'n' Softball game at USC's Dedeaux Field in front of a sell-out crowd of 3,500.

mid 89

Vince has a cameo role as a rock star in the Police Academy 6 movie but his scene is cut from the final version as they have too much footage overall.

One Sunday night, Nikki and Tommy have dinner with Bob Rock in Los Angeles. A glass of wine with their food turns into the rest of the bottle and before long Nikki phones a dealer. They go to a club for more drugs, girls and debauchery, before Bob gets them out of trouble by taking them back to A&M Studios where they carve swastikas into the walls.

Pretty Boy Floyd releases a cover of Mötley's Toast of the Town on their Leather Boyz With Electric Toyz album.

A Los Angeles radio station falsely announces the Crüe will play at the Roxy. The following Wednesday, a thousand people cue up around the corner of the venue, hoping to see the band.

Former Sex Pistols guitarist Steve Jones releases his new album titled Fire And Gasoline. The second track called We're Not Saints is written by Nikki with Steve Jones, along with his bass player Terry Nails.

The second album from German metal band Craaft, titled Second Honeymoon and released on RCA Records, thanks Tommy for his contribution.

11/7/89

Nominees for the MTV Video Awards are announced by Vince and Arsenio Hall during a press conference at the Saxonlee Art Gallery in Los Angeles. While back in Los Angeles, Vince undergoes surgery to correct a diagnosed deviated septum, which had been causing his face to swell over his years of alcohol and substance abuse.

With an abundance of tracks recorded in Vancouver, Mötley Crüe considers releasing two separate albums in quick succession, since they are contractually prohibited from releasing a double album. Nikki says the likely album title of the second release would be Mötley Crüe: The Ballads. Its release is primarily dependent on the success or failure of their next album.

8/89

Mötley manager Doc McGhee is in the final stages of putting together a huge rock concert in Moscow, through his Make A Difference Foundation, to commemorate the twentieth anniversary of Woodstock. Each band will play a fifty-minute set, stripped down with no props, pyrotechnics or special effects, and there will be no headlining act. The running order is to be Scorpions, Ozzy Osbourne, Mötley Crüe and Bon Jovi to finish the show. All proceeds from the two-day concert are to benefit anti-drug and alcohol charities.

Nikki now sports a new full sleeve of tattoos down his right arm; one of the first rock stars to do so. The band flew Sunset Strip Tattoo artist Greg James up to Vancouver for five days while recording the new album, and he effectively turned his hotel room into a tattoo studio.

12/8/89

Mötley plays a forty-five-minute set at the Moscow Music Peace Festival for their first-ever sober performance. Prior to the show, the concert's Production Manager tells Mötley they have been demoted in the line up, which makes Tommy livid that Doc's newer client in Bon Jovi is getting favoured over them and Scorpions, who are very popular in Russia. Nikki and Tommy tell Doc they are going home since they are not going to be an opening act for Bon Jovi's ninety-five-minute set, but they end up sorting the issue out and playing ahead of Ozzy. The concert draws an attendance of more than 100,000 and is watched by a worldwide television audience of a billion people.

At the start of Bon Jovi's set to finish off the night, a huge amount of pyro explodes. Knowing that permits would have needed to have been organised well beforehand, Tommy finds Doc backstage and punches him. While he is lying on the ground, Nikki tells him that he is fired as Mötley's manager since it's the second time he has outright lied to them about details of the concert.

13/8/89

On completion of the second day's performance in Moscow, Mötley flies back to Los Angeles via France and New York. Having now split with Doc McGhee as their manager, they encourage his partner Doug Thaler into also splitting from McGhee Entertainment, Inc. and managing them as his own company's first client. Doug agrees and soon forms his business called Top Rock Development Corporation.

Once back in Los Angeles, Vince goes on a ten-day white-water rafting trip down Idaho's Snake River. He calls Sharise on his way home who tells him of an altercation she just had with Izzy Stradlin' of Guns N' Roses at the Cathouse club. After trying to advance on Sharise and being turned down, saying she was married to Vince, Stradlin' pulled her top down in front of many people. Sharise slapped him in the face but then he kicked her in the stomach.

28/8/89

For the second successive time, the title track to the new Crüe album is released as the first single. This time it's Dr. Feelgood with Sticky Sweet as the B-side track. It's Mötley's first Top Ten hit, climbing as high as number six and charting for sixteen weeks, the longest of any Mötley single to date. The video for Dr. Feelgood is shot in a large aeroplane hangar in Pomona, California and has a feel similar to the movie Scarface. Mick's original riff for the song was titled Planet 9 from Outer Space. Sticky Sweet was the last song written for the album, with the lyrics being penned in the studio in supposedly less than a minute.

1/9/89

Mötley Crüe's fifth album is released, titled Dr. Feelgood. Costing around $600,000 to produce, it features guest appearances by members of Skid Row, Aerosmith, Cheap Trick, along with Jack Blades and Bryan Adams, who Tommy first met in a Vancouver strip club while recording the album. Cover artwork was originally going to have band mascot Allister Fiend drawn as a mad doctor holding a big syringe by the character's longtime artist Mike "Miq" Willmott. However, the final design of a dagger and a snake is a piece of tattoo flash, designed by Sunset Strip Tattoo artist Kevin Brady, who also designs the new Mötley Crüe logo. The forty-two-second opening track T. n T. (Terror 'n Tinseltown) was made by recording ambulance officers talking into their walkie-talkies, followed by driving their ambulance back and forth across the recording studio's car park.

5/9/89

Mötley presents the award for Best Heavy Metal Album at the MTV Music Video Awards at the Universal Amphitheatre in Universal City, California. While the rest of the Crüe waits in limos outside the event, Vince waits backstage while Guns N' Roses plays with Tom Petty. Vince then decks guitarist Izzy Stradlin' with a punch in the face as he comes off stage, as payback for recently hitting on then kicking his wife at the Cathouse. Mötley's security chief drags Vince away and as they are about to leave the building, Axl Rose tells Vince he is going to kill him. When Vince encourages him to bring it on, Axl walks away.

This is the start of a feud between the two bands. Axl Rose starts to say in the press that Vince sucker-punched Izzy and he has been insulting Guns N' Roses for years. Vince feels betrayed after showing Axl vocal tricks to help him out, while they supported Mötley on the Girls, Girls, Girls tour. Axl challenges Vince by sending at least six messages to fight at places like Tower Records in Los Angeles, or on the boardwalk at Venice Beach, but Axl never shows up. Meanwhile Izzy calls Vince and apologises for his behaviour.

Still angry at the incident and the way Axl has handled it via the press, Vince responds on MTV, telling Axl to name the place and time. After chatting with his friend and owner of the LA Lakers Jerry Buss, Vince proposes a Monday night three-round fight at the Great Western Forum in Los Angeles. Eddie Van Halen and Sammy Hagar from Van Halen say they'll put up the money to stage the fight at New York's Madison Square Gardens. No fight eventuates and Vince's offer still stands to this day.

11/9/89

Dr. Feelgood is released in Australia.

3/10/89

On Tommy's twenty-seventh birthday he receives a phone call from Ray DiMano at Elektra telling him that he finally has a number one album on the charts in Dr. Feelgood.

5/10/89

Mötley plays a 150-minute Dr. Feelgood warm-up show at the Whisky under their pseudonym The Foreskins, which is also used for the filming of their next video, Kickstart My Heart. Arriving at the venue in a vintage ambulance driven by rock comedian Sam Kinison, they play their first club gig since the early days. The set includes songs from Too Fast For Love previously never performed live. Photos from the night are also used in the Dr. Feelgood tour book. Bobby Oberdorsten becomes Mick's new guitar tech.

14/10/89

The European leg of the Dr. Feelgood tour starts in Essen, Germany, once again with the Nasty Habits on board and this time with Skid Row in support. It was decided Europe should be the first region to tour this album, since they missed out on the Girls, Girls, Girls tour following its cancellation. Before the Crüe enters the stage, Frank Zappa's song Crew Slut from his Joe's Garage Volume 1 album is played to the audience.

Vince throws beds out of a hotel window onto a couple of Mercedes cars parked below. German police search the hotel for the culprit with Uzi guns and Rottweiler dogs.

21/10/89

In Amsterdam, Nikki sees a she-male beat up a junkie. He is surprised by everyone smoking hash in coffee shops. People come up to him on the street with heroin, cocaine, and ecstasy. He buys some animal, dwarf and scat movies to show the others. The band members go to a live sex show where a guy, with track marks up and down his arms and a tattoo of a syringe on his foot, has sex with a chick right in front of them. A black lady has guys eating a bratwurst out of her vagina.

10/89

Vince spends four or five days filming in Denver, Colorado at Redrocks for a movie The Adventures of Ford Fairlane. Vince plays a rock star named Bobby Black from a band called Black Plague. Drummer Randy Castillo also acts as a member of Black Plague, along with Phil Soussan on bass. After Vince is killed in the movie's plot, an investigation starts into his death. The movie also stars Andrew Dice Clay, Robert Englund (Freddy Krueger from Nightmare on Elm Street), Ed O'Neill (Al Bundy from Married With Children), Wayne Newton and Priscilla Presley. Mötley Crüe writes and records the track called Rock N' Roll Junkie for the soundtrack. It was the last song recorded, along with the Tommy Bolin classic Teaser, before they left Little Mountain Studios in Vancouver.

The first printing of Revolutionary Comics Inc.'s "Rock 'n' Roll Comic - Mötley Crüe" is released.

11/89

A report surfaces that Matthew Trippe has dropped his lawsuit, which turns out to be false.

2/11/89

Dr. Feelgood becomes Mötley Crüe's first single to achieve Gold status, while the album now achieves double-Platinum status having sold two million copies in the U.S.

6/11/89

Mötley's European tour concludes in Scotland. On arrival back in the U.S. the Crüe rehearses on stage at the San Diego Sports Arena for five days.

15/11/89

With Mötley's continued success, their second album from six years ago, Shout At The Devil, now achieves triple-Platinum status.

16/11/89

The U.S. Dr. Feelgood tour starts in Tucson, Arizona and is set to continue through until April next year before heading overseas. An aeroplane for the tour is leased from a charter company in Texas owned by Tommy Beal; the same plane Def Leppard used and called Hystouria #1 on their Hysteria tour. The 21-seat G-159 Gulfstream 1 plane built by Grumman in 1960 receives a facelift to emblazon it with the Mötley Crüe logo on the fuselage as part of a black with purple paint job. The turbo-prop plane is also decked out with a mini recording studio inside its plush interior. A huge stereo system is built into the plane's walls, as are numerous colour TVs, a laser disc player and a video machine. Thirty-six Marshall stacks and thirty six SVT stacks accompany Mötley on the tour. An impressive laser light show is also used, similar to the one used in Neil Diamond's recent concerts.

The tour also sees an innovative and breathtaking drum solo from Tommy Lee on a new contraption, again built by former navy submarine hydraulics specialist Chris Deiter. As Mick finishes his guitar solo, Tommy holds onto a bungee rope before being slowly pulled up to the top of the venue by a chain motor. He then takes his place in a flying drum kit with electronic pads and huge speakers, which moves along hidden tracking while he plays along to some of his favourite rock songs. The medley includes Houses Of The Holy then Kashmir by Led Zeppelin, Rocky Mountain Way by Joe Walsh, Rock and Roll Hoochie Koo by Rick Derringer, Back in Black by

AC/DC, California Man by Cheap Trick, Ballroom Blitz by the Sweet and Back In The Saddle by Aerosmith. After bringing the show closer to the people at the back of the venue, his contraption turns around and he heads back towards the stage. Tommy triggers a sampled sound of a long descent as he puts his foot in a strap and grabs the rope again, before free-falling and stopping a few feet above the heads of the people nearest the front of the stage. Once back up on stage, he removes his braces one at a time before quickly downing his leather g-string and mooning the audience.

19/11/89
Tommy participates in a promotional motorcycle ride-a-thon called Love Ride 6 from Glendale to Malibu in benefit of the Muscular Dystrophy Association. He also drums on the song Shocker performed by The Dudes Of Wrath on the Shocker movie soundtrack. The song also features Paul Stanley from Kiss and Desmond Child on lead vocals, Whitesnake's Rudy Sarzo on bass, and Vivian Campbell on lead guitar with Kiss' Bruce Kulick, who is not credited on the album's liner notes.

20/11/89
Mötley Crüe's Kickstart My Heart single is released backed with She Goes Down. Like their previous single, it also spends a total of sixteen weeks on the U.S. charts, but only reaches number twenty six. Footage from their warm-up show at the Whisky is used for the video, mixed in with high-speed motor racing thrills and spills action. The zipper noise heard at the start of She Goes Down was sampled from a porno movie by Tommy. Twenty years later Vince says, "There's some sex being done in the background if you listen real closely. We can't say who's doing it though, but prostitution is legal in Vancouver."

26/11/89
Following their performance at Riverfront Coliseum, Tommy is cited by Cincinnati police for disorderly conduct after he dropped his leather g-string and mooned over twelve thousand

people in the crowd. The misdemeanour charge comes with a maximum fine of $113 that can be paid without appearing in court.

12/89

Mötley contributes their Vancouver recorded cover of ex-Deep Purple member Tommy Bolin's song Teaser to the Make A Difference Foundation's Stairway To Heaven/Highway To Hell album. They also feature on a cover of Led Zeppelin's classic song Rock N Roll with Skid Row, Zakk Wylde and Jason Bonham, recorded back in August at the Moscow Music Peace Festival.

A song called LA Jets written by Nikki Sixx and Lizzie Grey when they were together in their band London before the formation of Mötley Crüe is included on the second album from Lizzie's new band Ultra Pop, titled Adventures in Fantasy.

In hometown Los Angeles, a huge billboard reads "Have a Mötley Christmas and a Happy Crüe Year!" as part of Elektra's marketing efforts.

10/12/89

The Crüe plays a huge sell-out show at Meadowlands Arena in New Jersey. The encore includes Jailhouse Rock with Sebastian Bach from Skid Row, Dimebag Darrell from Pantera, Ace Frehley from Kiss and Ace's friend Gordon Gebert on keyboards.

Mötley finishes the decade in a powerful position within the music industry, having enjoyed success throughout their formative years in the 1980s.

Continue reading the story in these other books available in this series by Paul Miles:

Chronological Crue Vol. 2 - The Nineties
The complete history of Mötley Crüe in the 1990s

Chronological Crue Vol. 3 - The Naughties
The complete history of Mötley Crüe in the 2000s

Chronological Crue Vol. 4 - The Onesies
The ongoing history of Mötley Crüe in the 2010s

Acknowledgements

Tommy Lee, Mick Mars, Vince Neil, and especially Nikki Sixx: None of this would be possible without you guys of course. Thank you again for all the good, the bad, and the ugly over so many years now… much love and respect always. Rock 'n' roll forever!

Thanks also to former band members John Corabi and Randy Castillo (R.I.P.) for helping to give the band longevity when faced with challenges.

A Platinum-sized thank you to the Mötley Crüe management team at Tenth Street Entertainment, in particular Jeff Varner and Jordan Berliant, and in more recent years Chris Nilsson.

Thanks to the record company skinny cats: Dana Smart, Jeff Fura, and Petrina Convey down under. Great working with you in the past, I'm looking forward to more projects in the future.

Thanks very much to all the fans around the world who have contributed to the documented history by emailing me information and adjustments, both large and small, to help make Chronological Crue the mega-Mötley reference that it is today – it's *always* appreciated!

To Neil Strauss – I'm glad you emailed me all those years ago and I was able to get involved with what has turned out to be so many people's favourite book of all time. You know how to play The Game and are not backwards in coming Foreword. Thanks very much and see you soon.

A shout out to MTV's crazy Steve-O and Nicke Borg & Dregen of the Backyard Babies for their loving voiceovers for Chronological Crue. Thanks also to Steve-O for his testimonial in the front of this book, along with Rich Wilkes – let's hope your movie takes that dirty little book to the next level it deserves!

Much love to my wife Sara Miles for your days-upon-days of proof-reading and evaluation work on these books, over many months. I couldn't do all this without you by my side.

Thanks to those who have kindly participated in interviews with me over the years for publication on the Chronological Crue website; sharing their unique views and perspectives on the band, the music, the image, the lifestyle, the consequences and much more. This includes: Vinnie Chas (R.I.P.), Bill Larson (R.I.P.), Neil Zlowzower, Mike Flaherty, John Corabi, Athena Kottak, Neil Wharton, Allan Fryer (R.I.P.), Lita Ford, Randy Castillo (R.I.P.), Doc McGhee, Greg James, Neil Strauss, Stormy Deal, James Alverson, Will Boyett, Gordon Gebert, Mike 'Live Wire' Gallagher, and Roger Hemond.

To old pals Oretha Winston for her early assistance with Billboard chart data, Anders Nillson for kick-starting the Gigography concert listing way back in 1998, and Jen Genadry for her assistance and inspiration with the original Holiday L.A. tour guide that many fans have now traversed and enjoyed.

Horns-up to all the Crüeheads who have taken inspiration from the world of Mötley Crüe and adorned their bodies with a life long dedication – thanks for sending in the stories and photos of your Mötley tattoos for display in the Fan Ink gallery. The Crüe is with us forever!

Thanks to Shaun Pollitt at motley.com for his good-natured, competitive spirit, as we shared somewhat of an aligned journey from opposite ends of the Earth.

Last, but not least – you! Thanks for your loyal support of the website and the Crüe, and for purchasing this book – I trust you've enjoyed it and now value it as part of your Mötley Crüe collection.

About the Author

Paul Miles is the world's #1 Mötley Crüe historian, documenting the facts behind the band's "sex, drugs & rock'n'roll" lifestyle since 1995.

The pages of his acclaimed Chronological Crue website have literally been read millions and million times, following its launch on January 27, 1997 – the day vocalist Vince Neil reunited with the Crüe on stage at the American Music Awards.

Chronological Crue has been featured in many newspapers and publications around the world, including Japan's *Bass Magazine*, *Penthouse* magazine, hard rockers' favourite *Metal Edge*, and even the band's own Electronic Press Kit.

MTV & VH1 have both drawn upon and credited the site for their production of TV programs on Mötley Crüe, while music industry journalists, authors and critics continue to use his works as an invaluable reference on the band.

Paul Miles was Executive Producer of the award-winning, world's-first Mötley Crüe tribute CD, released with a Global Broadcast Premiere on the world's largest online radio station. Later in 1999, Miles was honoured to write the liner notes inside Mötley Crüe's first-ever live album - *Live: Entertainment or Death*.

After unsuccessfully pitching to band management the idea of turning his history content into a book a few years earlier, Paul Miles was engaged in 2001 to analytically assess the manuscript of the band's autobiography as it was in production.

The Dirt then spent a record amount of time on the New York Times Bestseller List, and the infamous story has been turned into a Netflix movie of the same name. Miles assisted the movie's screenwriter in verifying the accuracy of his script.

He was fortunate enough to tour the Crue's concerts around Australia in 2005 (read his book on that) and through Asia in 2008, as well as being there at the band's final ever shows that took place in Los Angeles, which concluded on New

Year's Eve 2015 (you can see his talking cameo appearance in *The End: Live in Los Angeles* concert DVD release.)

Paul Miles lives on a rainforest mountain-side just outside Melbourne, Australia, and when he's not in front of his computer, he can usually be seen in the photo pit of the city's rock concerts as he captures all the action with his cameras.

Read more about Paul Miles and his projects at www.Paul-Miles.com

Have you got these other rock'n'roll books by Paul Miles?

Sex Tips From Rock Stars
In Their Own Words
www.SexTipsFromRockStars.com

Before I Hit The Stage
Rock'n'Roll Moments in New York City
www.BeforeIHitTheStage.com

As you've read in the acknowledgements inside these books:

THE DIRT by Mötley Crüe & Neil Strauss:
"The biggest thanks of all goes to the tireless legions of Crueheads, specifically Paul Miles of Chronological Crue, whose list of corrections was almost as long as this book."

TATTOOS & TEQUILA by Vince Neil & Mike Sager:
"Special admiration and thanks to Paul Miles, curator of Chronological Crue, recognised worldwide as the ultimate Mötley Crüe historian."

KICKSTART MY HEART by Martin Popoff:
"I wish to acknowledge the immense Mötley Crüe scholarship and research of Australian expert Paul Miles, whose site Chronological Crue served as a dependable corroboration and fact-check resource as this book came together."

Printed in Great Britain
by Amazon